Crafting a
DISCIPLE

Don McCain

WordCrafts

Crafting a Disciple
Copyright © 2014
Don McCain

Cover design by David Warren
Front cover photo by Kenn Stilger
Author photo by Benjamin McCain

All rights reserved. No part of this book may be reproduced, stored in a retrieval system, or transmitted in any form or by any means – electronic, mechanical, photocopy, recording, or otherwise – without the prior written permission of the publisher. The only exception is brief quotations for review purposes.

Unless otherwise noted, all scripture quotations are taken from the American Standard Bible (Public Domain)

Scripture quotations marked KJV are taken from The Holy Bible, King James Version (Public Domain)

Scriptures taken from the Holy Bible, New International Version®, NIV®. Copyright © 1973, 1978, 1984, 2011 by Biblica, Inc.™ Used by permission of Zondervan. All rights reserved worldwide. www.zondervan.com The "NIV" and "New International Version" are trademarks registered in the United States Patent and Trademark Office by Biblica, Inc.™

Published by WordCrafts Press
Tullahoma, TN 37388
www.wordcrafts.net

Contents

Chapter 1
My Own Crafting 3

Chapter 2
Go and Make Disciples 11

Chapter 3
What Does The Word *Disciple* Mean? 15

Chapter 4
Matthew 28:18-20 Defined 20

Chapter 5
Baptized in the Father 24

Chapter 6
Baptized In The Son 37

Chapter 7
Embracing The Person Of The Holy Spirit 57

Chapter 8
The Holy Spirit Is Truth 65

Chapter 9
The Holy Spirit Is Power 70

Chapter 10
Concerning Spiritual Gifts 76

Chapter 11
How To Know The Voice Of God 99

Chapter 12
Be Strong In The Lord 114

Chapter 13
Build A Strong House 120

Chapter 14
The Life Of Prayer 125

Preface

Many religious groups today are of the impression that all you have to do is believe on the Lord Jesus Christ and you become a disciple. To believe on the Lord Jesus Christ will get you into His family but it will not make you a disciple. This book will define and instruct new believers on how to become true followers of Christ. This book is for helping those who have believed and do believe Jesus is the Christ to become solid followers of Christ. My hope is to strengthen believers in their relationship with God and others for the glory of God's Kingdom.

Jesus went about teaching that the kingdom of God is at hand. Did He mean God was showing up soon, or was He saying if you embrace me I will teach you the ways of my Father's Kingdom?

This is the journey we will take in this book, discovering the power of the Kingdom of God that has come to us through the person of Jesus Christ. Hopefully you will be enlightened to the truth of becoming true disciples of Christ. Once you know how to grow and follow Christ, you will be able to share what you have found with others. Pass this book on, or better still, invite new believers to your home and make disciples of them using this book as an instrument of teaching. The fastest growth of the kingdom today is in small home groups throughout the world. We need other believers and they need us.

Chapter 1
My Own Crafting

Disciples are made, not born - this is important to remember. When a person receives Christ it is only the beginning of their spiritual journey, not the complete deal.

A newborn baby knows nothing, but it needs loving arms that hold it. In the same way when new believers first come to Christ, when they are *born again*, they need loving arms to hold them. They need to feel the love of Jesus. That love usually that comes from those involved in providing pastoral care. In other words, they need to feel the love of those who will be providing spiritual nourishment, as caretakers or parents in Christ.

I intentionally chose the term, *crafting* a disciple, for the title of this book, rather than the more commonly used term, *making* a disciple, because I wanted to show the importance of what we hope to accomplish. A craftsman is one who knows a trade well; a person who is an expert in their field. As believers in Christ, we need to be *skilled* at the things of God - workman who are capable of presenting a beautiful and complete product.

But no one is a *born* craftsman. These skills must be learned. To accomplish God's purpose we must become masters of our craft, and to do that we must learn from a master craftsman.

Jesus, the Son of God, was also the son of a master craftsman, Joseph - a carpenter. No doubt Joseph learned his trade while serving as an apprentice to a mentor. In addition to learning the trade of a carpenter from his earthly father, Jesus was a craftsman of the things of His Heavenly Father. As a master craftsman, He called apprentices to Himself and mentored the twelve disciples. They called Him *Rabbi*, which means *Teacher*.

In the same way, we are called to both build and to be built up. The only way to become a craftsman who is skilled at both building and being built is to sit at the feet of teachers or Rabbis. We all need someone to coach us. We need to be apprenticed.

I taught my three oldest boys how to be carpenters, how to build and remodel residential and commercial buildings. They became so good at their trade they presently run a large construction company and train others to be skilled workers in that trade. They have grown into master craftsmen. Now they are coaches. They are mentors.

Their mother and I taught them the ways of Christ. We mentored them in Christ and now they are mentoring others in the faith. My wife and I have taught and mentored young people all our married lives, and some of those young people have gone on to become missionaries and pastors. Our purpose was to craft disciples who would become skilled in coaching others into the faith, and then they could help others to become craftsman of the faith. This is the heart of the Great Commission. In the Gospel of Matthew, chapter 28, Jesus commanded His followers to go into all the world and make, *or craft*, disciples. The Master went on to say that if we do all He commanded, He would be with us even to the end of the earth. He will still be our coach, Rabbi, teacher, mentor, day after day, until He brings us to completion.

We were not called to be spectators of the game of life, but players. Indeed we are called to play that game as experts. The scriptures refer to it as living an *abundant* life, a *victorious* life. But just like excelling at any skill requires work, having the abundant life means being committed to learning - and to never stop learning as we continue along our journey.

I have had great coaches along the way who have helped me to be strong in the Lord and the power of His might. My own personal crafting came through a *divine appointment*. If you're not familiar with that term, it simply means the Lord connected me with the right people at the right time. He is totally involved in causing intersections in our lives that will bring good to us.

The first divine encounter was my conversion experience, followed by the Lord arranging for me to come into contact with my *spiritual parents*. Spiritual parents are people the Lord places in your life to teach you the basics of the faith, to encourage your walk in the Lord and to disciple you. They are charged by God with the task of nourishing you in the things of the Spirit.

They are your tutors. You will certainly have other instructors in your life, but your spiritual parents are among the most important when it comes to crafting your faith.

I will share my own example of learning from my spiritual parents, so you can understand what I am talking about.

I can only describe my conversion experience as profound. I felt God's great love daily and desired Him greatly. But I was like a newborn babe, with no ability to care for myself in spiritual matters. I did not know what to do next. Our Heavenly Father knew this, so He had planned a divine appointment to get me into a home with people who became my spiritual parents.

You might remember the words to the beloved old hymn, "Amazing Grace." *I once was lost but now I am found/ was blind but now I see.* Those words were surely true for me. I needed help to see clearly - and so do you. I mean what do baby Christians eat, how do they get dressed, how do they walk and not get weary and run and not faint? The truth is, we all need people who are more mature in the faith, who can guide us until we can walk for ourselves and see for ourselves.

I had a lot to learn. In my first few months as a new babe in Christ I was like an orphan left on a door step of an orphanage. I couldn't even reach the doorbell to get help. I was totally dependent on someone to open the door, find me, and bring me in.

This is how I met my spiritual parents. I pulled into a gas station in the small town I grew up in. The gas station attendant, a friend of mine named Dale Hewitt, came to my driver's side window.

"Fill 'er up?" he asked. That was in the days of full service gas stations.

Dale, walking up to my window, was a divine appointment, arranged by our Father in heaven. He told me all the wonderful things the Lord was doing in his life and how he and his mother had been praying for me.

The Holy Spirit, Who was alive in Dale, was reaching out and touching me deep inside. That was all I could take. Like a baby hungry for food, I began to weep.

"What's wrong?" Dale asked.

"I have just received Jesus in my heart," I sobbed, "and don't know what to do."

"That's okay," he grinned at me. "My mom can fix that. Here is my address. Come over tonight at 6:00. We'll have some eats, and then we'll have all night to talk about Jesus."

There was already a small group of young adults gathered there by the time I arrived at Dale's house. We got acquainted over what Dale and I called "hubcap pizzas" - small frozen pizzas that would burn a little and become as hard as a hub cap.

Dale's mom, Coretta, taught the Word to us, starting with the basics. I had never heard God's Word so easily explained. Night after night we gathered to listen, break bread and fellowship. Coretta was crafting us into disciples through the truth of God's Word.

She wasn't in a hurry; she took her time and answered all our questions. She fed us the milk of the Word, then the meat. Coretta was building us into strong followers of Christ. She understood that disciples are not born, they are made. She was making disciples.

As a result of her patient efforts, we have carried on her work of making disciples for over forty years. She taught us how to know the Father, the Son and the Holy Spirit. She taught us the truth and strength of God's Word. She taught us how to know the voice of God. And she didn't try to do it all alone. Coretta took us to gospel meetings to hear others who were strong in the faith. She shared messages on tape from other ministers. She was truly faithful to her Lord Jesus Christ and His command to go and make disciples.

I hope you can see from my story the importance of spiritual parents, small groups, close friends and good shepherds or pastors. God puts these people in our lives to help craft us into strong followers of Christ. The Word tells us not to forsake assembling together; we need the family of God to help complete us.

Not only did I have Coretta as a mentor, I had her son as a best friend to share with on my own level. I had a pastor that pushed me on to Bible College where I discovered new friends in the faith and new tutors in Christ. I also found the second love of my life, my wife Patti. She has helped me grow even more in this journey of discipleship.

Nourishment for the Journey

Matthew 28:18-20 - *And Jesus came to them and spake unto them, saying, All authority hath been given unto me in heaven and on earth. Go ye therefore, and make disciples of all the nations, baptizing them into the name of the Father and of the Son and of the Holy Spirit: teaching them to observe all things whatsoever I commanded you: and lo, I am with you always, even unto the end of the world.*

Chapter 2
Go and Make Disciples

This is a text book on making disciples. Jesus, in Matthew 28:18-19 said, *Go into all the world and make disciples.* This is the imperative command to all believers, yet it is overlooked by many. I wrote this book as an instruction manual for making disciples and the simplicity of doing the work of an evangelist.

Jesus believed standing up for the kingdom of God was very important. He tells us in Matthew 10:32, 33 *Every one therefore who shall confess me before men, him will I also confess before my Father who is in heaven. But whosoever shall deny me before men, him will I also deny before my Father who is in heaven.*

These are powerful words. Thinking about the implications ought to be enough for every believer to take seriously the importance of sharing their faith. These words are one of the foundational pillars of our faith. They have been taught in the church for centuries, but I don't hear it from many pulpits today.

Have we replaced the responsibility of sharing the cross of Jesus Christ and His message with coffee in the house and a feel-good Gospel? Do we run from church to church looking for greater 'spiritual' thrills or happy feelings? Don't get me wrong. Fellowshipping around a cup of coffee is not a bad thing, but don't mistake it for making disciples. This gospel of Christ was preached by those who preceded us at a great cost - sometimes at the cost of their lives.

These great men and women of the Church were tortured and killed because they refused to be silent believers. They were disciples of the cross. They would not deny Christ, but lived to share Him every moment. They were a threat to the kingdom of darkness.

Jesus commanded us, the body of Christ, to go into the entire world and proclaim the Good News - *"the Kingdom of God is at hand!"* When this gospel is preached in the entire world as a witness, then the end will come.

The coming of His kingdom to earth will be the direct result of the gospel being witnessed in the entire world.

You are a witness. You have seen the power of God in your own life. You have experienced the anointed work of the Holy Spirit as the yoke of sin was broken in your life. Since you are a witness, you are called to testify, to preach and proclaim what you have seen, heard and experienced. The great thing is that you are not alone in your testimony. The Bible declares that His Word will not to return void, but accomplish what He sends it forth to do.

Crafting a Disciple has a double purpose. It is designed as a workbook on how to make disciples and on how to be a disciple. I hope it will inspire you to greater boldness in your faith in the good news of Jesus Christ. I hope it will encourage you to exercise His ability in you by the Holy Spirit. And I hope it will teach you to be a threat to the kingdom of darkness.

Let us determine to fully embrace the work of the cross, and pray for its effectiveness in us to be lights set on a hill for all to see.

Nourishment for the Journey

Matthew 10:32 - *Every one therefore who shall confess me before men, him will I also confess before my Father who is in heaven.*

Chapter 3
What Does The Word *Disciple* Mean?

Our word *disciple* comes from the Greek word *mathetes,* which means: pupil, apprentice, one who learns from a master. It is also the root for *math*, meaning the mental effort to think something through. A disciple is one who puts forth effort to learn something of great value, being taught by one who is accomplished in their field. This is why Jesus was called Rabbi (teacher); He was the master teacher of the ways of the Father's Kingdom.

Jesus told His followers, *I am the way, the truth, and the life.* True discipleship has nothing to do with the opinions others might have about what the Kingdom of God is. True discipleship involves seeing the Kingdom as it really is, through the eyes of Jesus.

As believers, we must become students of our master teacher, and learn of Him the true nature of the Kingdom of God.

It is fine to have an opinion about the Kingdom of God. Churches all over the world teach their opinion about the Kingdom. The question is, does that opinion line up with what Jesus says about the Kingdom? You see, Jesus does not have an opinion. He knows the truth of the matter. And He is, in fact, The Truth of the matter.

You might have heard the old saying, *God said it, I believe it, that settles it.* (And that old saying is true...as long as God really did *say it.* There are a lot of things we *think* God said that simply aren't in His Word.) It doesn't help to argue with God. He is always right, and that is the end of every argument. After all, He is God, and we're not. He is righteous in all His ways; we're not.

We are all like sheep who have gone astray, and without a shepherd we will continue to stray. As the old hymn writer proclaimed, *I once was lost but now I am found.* I needed to be found by the loving and caring Shepherd - and so do you.

God by His Word and the Holy Spirit removes the shackles - the chains we accepted by erroneous teachings - and delivers us to freedom. As the Word declares, *He who the Son sets free is free indeed.*

Education can be good or bad. There are thousands of books we can read and study on every subject known to man, but just because something is written down in a book doesn't make it true. An author's opinion does not necessarily make them an authority on the subject.

This is particularly true in the realm of theology and philosophy. People have gathered to themselves a multitude of teachers, because they have itching ears and desire to hear something new. These men and women may even think themselves to be an authority on the subject, but the absolute truth of all matters comes from God.

The One who created this world and all that is in it is the final authority.

I don't know about you, but I prefer to have someone *higher* than higher education as my tutor. If those whom I am told by the world to esteem are not disciples of the master teacher, Jesus Christ, their teaching is of no value, to me or to you.

The Spirit of God brings peace to our journey. If we are being discipled by teachers whose thoughts and ideas oppose His truth, we will walk in confusion and witchcraft, and we will have no peace. I have friends who have become disciples of all kinds of worldly thoughts, and they have no true peace. The problem is, they keep looking for Truth in all the wrong places.

With so many people saying so many different things, it's understandable that you can get confused. The Bible tells us in the last days men will run to and fro throughout the whole earth looking for wisdom and finding none. You might consider just throwing up your hands and saying, *Who can you believe*?

The first step in answering that question is understanding what it is you are looking for.

If my wedding ring gets knocked off the night stand and rolls under the bed, I have a good chance of finding it, partly because it is an object I am familiar with. I know what it looks like and I have a pretty good idea of the general area where it might be found. But if you ask me to help you look for your wedding ring, things get a bit more difficult, particularly if I've never seen your wedding ring, and you can't describe it, and you don't remember where you lost it.

It is the same principle with wisdom - if you've never been exposed to true wisdom, how will you know it when you encounter it?

Fortunately, God in His infinite kindness hardwired the ability to recognize His work and His Spirit into our DNA. You will know the Truth and the Truth will make you free. His Word and Spirit are the things God uses to reveal His Truth to the inner man. But you will never know this Truth I am speaking of until you take a step of faith and trust Him to reveal Himself to you.

All the book-learning in the world cannot reveal the things of the Spirit, because they *are* spirit. The Word tells us in I Cor. 2:10 that only the Spirit reveals the things of the Spirit.

Nourishment for the Journey

I Corinthians 2:10 - *But unto us God revealed them through the Spirit: for the Spirit searcheth all things, yea, the deep things of God.*

Chapter 4
Matthew 28:18-20 Defined

In the last chapter of the Gospel of Mathew, Jesus gave his followers one last, important command. *"All authority in heaven and on earth has been given to me,"* He declared. *"Therefore go and make disciples of all nations, baptizing them in the name of the Father and of the Son and of the Holy Spirit, teaching them to obey everything I have commanded you. And surely I am with you always, to the very end of the age."* (NIV)

We are going to dissect these verses and look at them in depth. First, consider what has taken place prior to these verses. Some of the disciples have visited the tomb where Jesus was buried following his crucifixion. They found it empty.

This is extremely important. In fact, it is the single most important event, not only in Christian history, but in the entire history of the human race. The tomb was empty! Jesus wasn't there. This one event, known as the resurrection, is unique and is the very thing that sets Christianity apart from all other religions. Every other founder of every other religion is dead…or will be one day. And they are all still in their graves. Jesus was proclaimed by God to be His one and only begotten Son, by the power that raised Him from the dead!

He appeared to His disciples for a period of time after His resurrection, encouraging them, teaching them and finally commanding them to do the same thing He had been doing all along - *"Go into all the world and make disciples."*

His command was two-part: 1) *Go* into *all* the world, and 2) M*ake* disciples of *all* nations.

Jesus commanded them, and us, to use His teachings to make learned ones; to reproduce in others what we have received. This was the mandate from the Master to his disciples, and it is still His mandate for His followers today. Go! Bring others into the Kingdom of God. Craft those followers into disciples, and teach them to go and make disciples of others - with the promise that Jesus Himself will be with us!

That brings up the question of just exactly how are we supposed to do this whole disciple-making thing? Fortunately, Jesus provides us with a very helpful instruction when He said to baptize them in the name of the Father, the Son and the Holy Spirit.

The people Jesus was physically talking to were very familiar with the concept of baptism. John the Baptist had spent his entire earthly ministry exhorting anyone who would listen to repent and be baptized for the remission of their sins. Jesus Himself was baptized by John, not that He had any sins that needed remission, but to fulfill all righteousness.

But I don't think water baptism is what Jesus is referring to in this passage.

Let me be very clear. Water baptism is a visible means of showing our commitment to Christ, and it is a good thing, a holy thing. In the book of The Acts of the Apostles, followers of Jesus were publicly baptized in water in the name of Jesus for the remission of their sins. Water baptism is a public response to becoming a believer and serves as a physical outward expression of the death, burial and resurrection of Christ to the world.

I have used these verses in Matthew 28: 18-19 when I've performed water baptisms and still do. But I believe Jesus had something deeper than water baptism in mind with this commandment. The command was to baptize them in the name of the Father and of the Son and of the Holy Spirit in relation to the subject of making disciples.

The literal meaning of the word 'baptism' is complete submersion or emersion. I believe when Jesus commanded His followers to be baptized in the name of the Father, Son and Holy Spirit, He wanted them, and us, to be fully submerged, emerged, saturated by and filled with God, the Trinity, the Three-In-One.

This is what we hope to do in the following chapters - to plunge you into an understanding of the Father, the Son and the Holy Spirit.

You may say, "I know who God is," or "I am a studier of the words of Jesus," or "I believe we get the Holy Spirit at conversion." All of those things may be true, but I would ask, "Are you one-dimensional or complete in your understanding of the Trinity? Are you completely full of God?"

This is one of the primary reasons why we have so many camps, or denominations, today. Each group focuses on one area of the Godhead. If we truly want to be complete in our discipleship training, we must embrace all three members of the Trinity as they relate to us.

How about this? Let's place our present understanding of God on the table for now. Let's start our journey toward becoming a disciple of Jesus together. Then let's work together to make new disciples. Let us covenant together to return to Matthew 28:18-20, to be baptized, or fully embrace, the persons of the Trinity so we can press on toward completion in becoming disciples.

Chapter 5
Baptized in the Father

What does Jesus' command to "...baptize in the name of the Father..." for making a disciple mean? How do we accomplish that?

Since we learned that *baptize* means *to plunge into, submerse ourselves in, to be engulfed by*, it stands to reason that being baptized in the name of the Father means we should be totally filled with all the knowledge of *who* the Father is and *what* our relationship to Him should be.

Jehovah God, or Yahweh as he was known in the Old Testament, was known as Creator, Ruler, King and Judge. But Jesus introduced a completely new understanding of the nature of God when He taught His disciples that God was also their Heavenly *Father*. While we might take that concept for granted, it was a radical idea during the 1st century A.D.

When Jesus told His disciples - His pupils - how to pray in Matthew 6:9, He instructed them to pray to, *"Our Father who is in heaven."* He wanted them to realize Jehovah wanted to have a personal relationship with them. He wasn't some powerful but obscure entity they could not know.

Jesus encouraged his disciples to have an intimate conversation with Jehovah, as if He really was your dad. Ask Him for your daily bread. Ask Him to direct your path away from sin and the evil one. Ask Him to lead you into paths of righteousness and to deliver you from temptation and the evil one.

But this conversation wasn't intended to be centered on you. It was all for God's glory. Jesus encouraged His disciples to let their light shine before men in such a way that they may *"see your good works and glorify your Father who is in heaven"* (Matthew 5:16). Jesus was training His followers to recognize that the great God Jehovah is their Abba Father.

The Greek word, *Abba*, is an intimate expression for *Father*, much like our terms *Daddy* or *Papa*. It is a loving expression used by a child who knows it is loved and cared for. When Jesus personalized our relationship with Jehovah God as one of a child to a loving, caring, ever-present Daddy, it put that relationship in a whole new light.

The reason we let our light shine is not to earn the praise of men for ourselves, but to bring attention to our connection with Jehovah as the head of our lives and our family. Jesus commanded us to do good works - works that point to the kingdom of God and not the kingdoms of this world. These works should be different. Our attitudes toward those works should be different. Instead of getting angry and being unforgiving, we must show mercy and extend forgiveness for wrongs done against us. Our ways should be noticeably different than those of the world around us. Our words and deeds should point to the greatness of our *Abba,* Father, who is God.

In the early days of our ministry, we called our evangelistic meetings, "My God is God." Our point was to declare that no one could accomplish the great feat of changing people's lives but our God. We wanted to make it perfectly clear that in addition to being an all-knowing, all-powerful God, our God is also a kind and loving Father.

There is a great story about a famous evangelist who had a powerful and fruitful ministry. During a conversation, another preacher commented to this great man of God, "I spend two hours a day in my secret prayer place, and looking at your ministry, it is obvious that you must do the same." "No," the humble evangelist replied. "I don't spend hours alone in a prayer closet. I just talk to my Father in heaven all day, then do what He tells me."

This is what Jesus was trying to convey to His disciples. Just keep an ongoing conversation with your heavenly Dad.

I know some people have a difficult time with this concept, either because they did not have an earthly father in their lives, or their relationship with their earthly father was not good. It's hard to imagine a kind and loving *heavenly* Father if your *earthly* father was unkind, unloving, abusive or absent.

For the benefit of those of you who have no personal experience to draw from, here are some traits of a good father. A father is one who protects. He is concerned about your welfare. A father takes care of his child's physical needs: shelter, clothing, food. A father is interested in educating the child in regards to all things that pertain to life: from teaching you how to walk and talk, to teaching you how to interact with other people. A father picks you up and holds you when you're hurt. A father chases away your enemies, fights your fights with and for you. A father is a friend you can talk to, who will listen and impart wisdom. A good father will discipline you when you stray from the path of life; not to harm you, but to keep you from harming yourself or others. In a nutshell, your earthly father should be a reflection of your heavenly father - a loving, protecting provider.

It is imperative that we see and accept Jehovah God as our Father, because that is how He has chosen to reveal Himself to us.

In addition to being a loving, protecting provider, our heavenly Father is also the best of friends. When I counsel couples for marriage, I share this about the husband's role: He is to be provider, protector and loving friend. These are also attributes Jesus told us about His Father which is in heaven.

Once again it's hard to draw on the world's model to reach a valid conclusion about the friendship of God. In many cases our examples of friends are not so good. We've all had fair-weather friends who deserted us when times got hard. Sometimes we've even been that friend who wasn't willing or able to live up to the expectations of true friendship.

But Jesus revealed God as a true friend Who would never leave or forsake us. Our Father in Heaven is not selfish. He is truly interested in our welfare. And we can trust Him completely, not only with our stuff and our relationships, but with our very lives. Why? Because He cares for us!

I Peter 5:7 commands us to cast all our cares and concerns upon Him because He cares for us. He knows what is going on in our lives and has our best outcome at heart. He will take your part in the matter. He wants to carry *all* of your cares.

In Ephesians 2:4-5, the Apostle Paul declared that it was because of God's rich mercy and great love that compelled Him to give us new life in Christ - not after we got our acts together - but while we were dead in our sins! He proved his desire to be our Father by sending His own Son to die on the Cross. It is the death, burial and resurrection of Jesus Christ that provided us the privilege of becoming sons and daughters of God.

I once heard a saying that I've used many times in my life that sums up how God feels about you and me: *If God, our Heavenly Father, had a refrigerator - your picture would be on it.*

That is a powerful image for me. Patti and I have pictures of all our children and grandchildren on our refrigerator, because we want to see them, multiple times, every day. And every time we look at one of those pictures, we smile.

Of course our Father in Heaven doesn't need a picture on a refrigerator to bring us to mind. He is mindful of us all day and all night, and when He thinks about us, I know he smiles. His Word tells us He knew us before we were even conceived in the womb. He knows how many hairs are on our heads. We were not accidents. He planned us from the foundation of the world. That makes us very special to Him. Why? Because He *is* our *Daddy* God.

The greatest New Testament verse, at least to my way of thinking, is John 3:16 - *"For God so loved the world that He gave His only begotten Son that whosoever believeth on Him should not perish but have eternal life."* It will take a lifetime for us to realize the impact of these words. Just think about how much the great God Jehovah loves us!

According to Paul's letter to the Ephesians, He has loved us before He laid the foundation of the world. Not only did He know us, but He chose us! He has been looking forward to you and me becoming His children for a long, long time. That should make you exceedingly glad.

Whatever your earthly circumstances might be - regardless of whether you had parents that loved you immensely or if your parents abandoned you to fend for yourself - you are greatly loved by God the Father.

He greatly desires to be your Father. Let Him be your *daddy*.

Psalm 34:15-22 declares that the eyes of the Lord are on the righteous; that He hears them, protects them and delivers them. Bottom line: Our Father in heaven has your back. He's looking out for you. He is interested in your success.

As a father, I would do anything within my power to help my children succeed in all of their endeavors. As much as I love my kids, God loves them even more. It's a crazy thought, but it's true. I know, because I have experienced it.

While Jesus referred to the great God Jehovah as Abba, *Daddy*, He has many other names. These names reference different attributes of His character.

Genesis 22 tells the story of Abraham preparing to sacrifice his son Isaac on the altar. As the great patriarch of the faith raised his knife to slay the boy, God stayed his hand, and even provided a ram, caught by its horns in the brush, to use as a sacrifice instead. Abraham referred to Him as **Jehovah Jireh** - God will provide.

We too can call on Jehovah Jireh to provide our needs. Jesus taught that God provides for the birds of the air and the flowers of the field. Surely, He said, we are worth much more than these. We as earthly parents want to give good things to our children. If they ask for bread, we wouldn't give them rocks to eat. Our heavenly Father is concerned with our daily needs, and He is trustworthy to meet all our needs.

Perhaps the most quoted passage from the Old Testament is the 23rd Psalm. David, the great Shepherd King of Israel, referred to God as **Jehovah Rohi** - The LORD is my Shepherd.

Shepherd is a wonderful picture of God's love, care and mercy, particularly since Christ so often referred to his followers as sheep. Sheep don't worry about their next meal, or where they are going tomorrow. David writes this psalm from the perspective of a sheep. Listen to how he describes the work of Jehovah Rohi: I shall not want. He is going to take care of all my needs. He makes me lie down in green pastures. He will lead me to good places of rest, abundance, safety and calmness. He leads me beside quiet waters. He is my calm in all things. He restores my soul. He puts my mind at peace and fills me with confidence. He guides me in the paths of righteousness. Even though I walk through the valley of the shadow of death, I will fear no evil, for He is with me.

Shepherds are not only providers and leaders; they are also protectors. Jesus declared Himself to be the Good Shepherd, then He went on to explain that the Good Shepherd lays down His life for the sheep. With all of these attributes it is no wonder our heavenly Father is referred to as Jehovah Rohi - our shepherd.

The Old Testament prophet, Jeremiah, foresaw the coming of the Messiah, and referred to Him as **Jehovah Tsidkenu** - the Lord our Righteousness.

Our Father God is Lord of Righteousness. He can only operate in righteousness or holiness. We should be keenly aware that whatever the LORD God does, that action is righteous and holy. If we think something that God does or says in His Word is wrong, we need to readjust our thinking. God will never act contrary to His nature, and His very nature is holy.

Because He is holy, He has commanded us to be holy. Therein, as the old saying goes, lies the rub.

We don't know how to be holy or righteous. Most of the time we don't want to be holy or righteous. And even when we do want to be holy and righteous, we may not know His voice well enough to follow Him, particularly when other voices that we know all too well are calling our names.

Thank God, He has made provision for that failing on our part. We'll get to that later in this book.

The Psalmist refers to our heavenly Father as **Jehovah Shammah** - the LORD is there - a very present help in times of trouble. He is always present. He is always there, as close as your next breath. Before Jesus ascended back to the Father after His earthly ministry was finished, He promised He would never leave us nor forsake us. Our God is Shammah - always present and always ready to help whenever we need Him. He's always present, even when we don't want Him. And He's always ready to help, even when we don't think we need Him.

The book of Exodus recounts the story of God's deliverance of the children of Israel from Egyptian bondage. Because of Pharaoh's hard heart, God had to send plagues upon Egypt, including horrendous diseases. The word of the Lord to Moses was, none of the plagues of Egypt will come upon the Hebrews because Jehovah is **Rapha** - their healer.

One of the most powerful ministries of Jesus during His time on earth was that of healing all manner of sickness. He healed the lame, the deaf, the blind. He raised the dead. He cleansed those afflicted with leprosy. The Word says Jesus went about doing good and healing all that were oppressed by the devil.

These are only a few examples of the names and attributes of our Father God. As children we used to brag about how strong our daddy was. We have a daddy in heaven, and our Daddy is stronger than the world's daddy. Our Father in heaven is the one and only true God, and He wants to be your champion.

Nourishment for the Journey

Matthew 5:16 - *Even so let your light shine before men; that they may see your good works, and glorify your Father who is in heaven.*

Matthew 6:9 - *After this manner therefore pray ye. Our Father who art in heaven, Hallowed be thy name.*

I Peter 5:7 - *Casting all your anxiety upon him, because he careth for you.*

Ephesians 2:4-5 - *But God, being rich in mercy, for his great love wherewith he loved us, even when we were dead through our trespasses, made us alive together with Christ (by grace have ye been saved).*

John 3:16 - *For God so loved the world, that he gave his only begotten Son, that whosoever believeth on him should not perish, but have eternal life.*

Ephesians 1:4 - *Even as he chose us in him before the foundation of the world, that we should be holy and without blemish before him in love.*

Psalm 34:15-22 - *The eyes of Jehovah are toward the righteous, And his ears are open unto their cry. The face of Jehovah is against them that do evil, To cut off the remembrance of them from the earth. The righteous cried, and Jehovah heard, And delivered them out of all their troubles. Jehovah is nigh unto them that are of a broken heart, And saveth such as are of a contrite spirit. Many are the afflictions of the righteous; But Jehovah delivereth him out of them all. He keepeth all his bones: Not one of them is broken.*

Evil shall slay the wicked; And they that hate the righteous shall be condemned. Jehovah redeemeth the soul of his servants; And none of them that take refuge in him shall be condemned.

Genesis 22:14 - *And Abraham called the name of that place Jehovah-jireh. As it is said to this day, In the mount of Jehovah it shall be provided.*

Matthew 6:26 - *Behold the birds of the heaven, that they sow not, neither do they reap, nor gather into barns; and your heavenly Father feedeth them. Are not ye of much more value then they?*

Psalm 23:1 - *Jehovah is my shepherd; I shall not want.*

John 10:11 - *I am the good shepherd: the good shepherd layeth down his life for the sheep.*

Jeremiah 23:6 - *In his days Judah shall be saved, and Israel shall dwell safely; and this is his name whereby he shall be called: Jehovah our righteousness.*

Psalm 46:1 - *God is our refuge and strength, A very present help in trouble.*

Psalm 37:25 - *I have been young, and now am old; Yet have I not seen the righteous forsaken, Nor his seed begging bread.*

Exodus 15:26 - *and he said, If thou wilt diligently hearken to the voice of Jehovah thy God, and wilt do that which is right in his eyes, and wilt give ear to his commandments, and keep all his statutes, I will put* *none of the diseases upon thee, which I have put upon the Egyptians: for I am Jehovah that healeth thee.*

Acts 10:38 - *Even Jesus of Nazareth, how God anointed him with the Holy Spirit and with power: who went about doing good, and healing all that were oppressed of the devil; for God was with him.*

Chapter 6
Baptized In The Son

We are studying what it means to make a disciple. Our key verse is Matthew 28:19, where Jesus commands His followers to go into all the world and make disciples, of all the nations, by baptizing them (plunging them into) the Father, the Son and the Holy Spirit.

The implication is that we must become drenched in, or fully soaked with, the knowledge and understanding of who these three are, and how they are to work in our lives. In the last chapter we discovered the nature of God the Father. In this chapter we will examine what it means to embrace, or be baptized into the Son. We'll learn what our relationship is to Jesus Christ.

One of the central tenants of the Christian faith is that Jesus is '*very God of very God.*' But He is also referred to in Scripture as the Son of the Living God. Jesus asked His disciples, 'Who do you say I am,' to which Simon Peter answered 'You are the Christ, the

Son of the Living God.' This wasn't just something Peter said off the top of his head. It was revelation from God, pure and simple. Jesus declared, 'Blessed are you Simon, for flesh and blood did not reveal this to you but my Father which is in heaven!'

His disciples weren't the only ones who acknowledged Jesus as the Son of God. In the Gospel of Matthew, 8:29, and again in Mark's Gospel, 11:23, demons acknowledged His authority over them, referring to Him as the Son of God. The angel who announced the incarnation to the Virgin Mary, told her the holy child she was to bear would be great and would be called the Son of God. Jesus's predecessor, John the Baptizer, who was sent to prepare the way of the Lord declared Him to be the Son of God. When Lazarus died, Jesus told the dead man's sisters, Mary and Martha, that the sickness was for the glory of God so that the Son of God (Himself) would be glorified. When the religious leaders of the day questioned Him and asked Him if He was the Son of God, Jesus replied, *"I Am!"* Even the centurion responsible for crucifying Him declared, *"This must truly be the Son of God."*

Another title bestowed upon Jesus was "the Christ." While it is common for us today to hear the name *Jesus Christ* spoken (sometimes as a blessing but unfortunately many times as a curse), you might not know what the word *Christ* actually means.

Contrary to popular belief, *Christ* is not Jesus' last name. Instead, *Christ* is a powerful and potent title.

To understand its meaning we have to go all the way back to ancient Israel. The nation of Israel was looking for a deliverer like Moses, a powerful one who was foretold by the prophets who would rebuild the temple, crush all of Israel's enemies and rule the land in righteousness and justice. This deliverer was referred to as the Messiah, the Anointed One, sent by Jehovah God to set up God's kingdom on earth. The Greek word *Christos*, from which we get our English word *Christ*, means *the Anointed One*. When we speak of Jesus *Christ*, we are calling Him the *Messiah*!

The problem is, the religious leaders of the first century were looking for a political and military leader. They certainly were not looking for a suffering savior like Jesus.

While many Jews did believe and became the first disciples, the Jewish nation as a whole did not accept Jesus as their Messiah, and today many of those of the Jewish faith still wait for the Messiah to come and deliver them. Those of us who hold to the Christian faith, Jews and Gentiles alike, accept Jesus as the Messiah, the Christ, the Anointed One. We know He came and that He has promised to return. We anxiously await His second coming when He will establish His Kingdom.

Jesus's title of Christ was announced on the day of his birth by angels. You might recall the story from Luke 2:11, or maybe from the Charlie Brown Christmas Special on TV - *"For unto you is born this day in the City of David a Savior, who is Christ the Lord."*

As the Christ, Jesus was endowed with all spiritual authority. Even demons were subject to his authority. According to Luke 4:41 the demons could not speak because they knew He was the Christ, the Anointed One, the All-Powerful One. They had to submit to His will because He was, and is, Lord.

The Apostle John said one reason he wrote down the signs, miracles and wonders that Jesus performed, was so those who read his Gospel "might believe that Jesus is the Christ."

Yes, Jesus is referred to in the Bible as the Son of God and as the Christ, but like the old TV commercial used to say - "But wait! There's more!"

John, the baptizer, saw Jesus coming and proclaimed to the crowd, *"Behold the Lamb of God that taketh away the sin of the world."* (John 1:29)

In the first chapter of his gospel, the Apostle John wrote that the Word became flesh and dwelt among us. John is very clear that this Word, referring to Jesus Christ, was with God from the beginning, and was in fact God, an integral part of the Trinity - separate, equal and one with God the Father and God the Holy Spirit.

As the eternal Word of God, He is the agent through which all things were created. The writer of of the New Testament book of Hebrews tells us that the worlds were framed by the Word of God. In the Genesis account of creation, when God said, "Let there be..." Jesus, as the Word of God, was the one doing the creating. In his second letter, the Apostle Peter declared not only were the heavens formed by the Word, but they are held together *to this day* by the Word of God.

Bottom line: nothing takes place on this planet unless He speaks it into being. That's our God, and that is pretty awesome!

Jesus referred to Himself as "the Way, the Truth and the Life" and went on to say that no one can come to the Father except through Him. He is the one and only bridge between sinful man and holy God.

Luke, the beloved physician, writes in the Acts of the Apostles, that Jesus is the all powerful Anointed One, and that he proved who He was by going about doing good, healing all kinds of diseases and delivering the oppressed.

The name of Jesus Christ is higher than any other name on earth, in heaven or under the earth. In his letter to the Philippians, the Apostle Paul declares Him to have the name that is above all names, and at His name every knee will bow and every tongue will confess that He is Lord, to the glory of God the Father.

In plain English, that means He has all authority over every created thing. He is greater than any political superpower. He is greater than any demon from hell or angel in heaven. And one of the coolest things about being a follower of Jesus Christ is - He shares that power and authority with us! As the Bible says, *"greater is He that is in you than he that is in the world."* The same power and anointing that raised Christ from the dead, by the Holy Spirit, is available to us as joint heirs with Jesus. (We will deal with our position in Christ in a later chapter.)

This is just one reason why it is so important to be very familiar with the Bible. To know the Word is to know Jesus. To embrace the Word is to embrace Jesus.

In his letter to the Romans, the Apostle Paul tells us that if you confess with your mouth that Jesus is Lord and believe in your heart that God raised him from the dead you shall be saved. We've already noted that we get to participate in the power and authority of Christ, but before you can exercise that authority, power and anointing, it must be transferred to us. That transfer of authority only comes by us accepting and acknowledging Jesus as our Lord and Master.

Trying to exercise the authority of Christ without the lordship of Christ in your life, would be like walking onto an Army post and ordering a company of soldiers to "Take the hill!" Those soldier wouldn't move because they don't recognize your authority to give an order. But if a crusty old First Sergeant barks out, "Take the hill!" you can bet the troops will snap to attention and obey. They recognize that the First Sergeant has been given authority to issue that order from someone who has even greater authority.

Making Jesus your Lord is about recognizing that we are weak. We are a fallen race of beings. We are unable to save ourselves, and desperately need His strength to save us from our fallen state of mind and actions.

This salvation is not something that we have the ability to earn apart from the work of Christ in our lives. And the work of Christ in our lives is solely through the grace of God that brings salvation. Doing good works is a wonderful thing, and as Christians we are certainly called to do good works so the world will see and give glory to God. But good works won't earn salvation. It is a gift from God because of His great love for us, a love we cannot even begin to comprehend.

Jesus purchased our redemption by the shedding of His own blood. He made the supreme sacrifice by willingly dying on a cross, a common form of execution for criminals during the days of the Roman Empire. The Apostle Paul tells us in his letter to the Romans that the wages of sin is death. Since we have all sinned, death is the ultimate outcome and payment for our sin. You could say we are indebted to sin and can only pay that debt by forfeiting our lives.

By dying on the cross, Jesus paid that debt for you and me and the whole world. Since Jesus committed no sin, He owed no debt. Yet He paid a debt He did not owe so we could be released from the penalty of death for our rebellion toward God and His kingdom.

It might sound like a high price to pay but the writer of the letter to the Hebrews declares that without the shedding of blood there is no remission of sin.

Jesus paid the full price for our sin, but in order to appropriate that life, the salvation that He purchased, we must fully embrace Him as our personal Lord and Master. A master is someone who has complete ownership over another person. But Jesus is not a master like we think of in the old plantation days. When we submit to the Lordship of Christ, we must do so willingly, not out of fear or compulsion.

There is no comparison to what the world shows us master and slave are like. Jesus is a Master who gave His life for me, who daily provides all I need spiritually and physically. His yoke is easy and His burden is light. He never punishes us if we miss the mark, but kindly and gently restores us into fellowship with Himself.

Don't misunderstand. If you do not choose to make Jesus your master; you still have a master, and that master is not kind. His yoke is harsh and his burden is heavy. If you refuse to make Jesus your Lord, and choose to live life on your own terms, there will be consequences.

This is just as true in the spiritual world as it is in the natural world. For example, on one occasion when I was a young driver, I saw a road sign that indicated a curve in the road up ahead. The speed limit for the curve was 25 mph. I did not heed that warning and took the curve at 50 mph. My car did not hold the road at that speed and the consequence for ignoring the sign was - I ended up in the ditch.

God did not put my car in the ditch. It was the natural consequence for ignoring the warning signs that were given to me. I put my car in the ditch because I thought I knew more than the highway department. I thought I could handle it. I thought it would be okay.

I was wrong, and I had to pay the consequence. I had to pay for hiring a tow truck to pull my car out of the ditch, and I had to pay for the damage to my car. It was only by God's infinite grace and mercy that I was protected from physical injury.

It seems we are always trying to do things our way, when we have a Master of all things that can help us avoid the troubles ahead. He knows everything. He sees way ahead of us, in regard to our lives and what is coming. He has placed warning signs and directional markers to help us reach our destination safely. His Word, the Holy Spirit, Godly leaders, elders and those saints who have walked this life before us are road signs He uses to guide us along the way.

With all these resources, why do we so often insist on going it on our own? Well, according to King Solomon in Proverbs 12:1, sometimes we're just too stupid to know better. Of course, Solomon put it a lot more poetically. He who rejects reproof is stupid, the wise king said.

The reverse is also true. As Solomon continues by saying, *"He who loves discipline, (you could just as easily say, He who is a disciple) loves knowledge."* Think about it: you can go your own way and be stupid, or you can embrace God's discipline and be wise.

If Jesus is who the Word of God says He is, *and He is*, doesn't it make sense to let him call the shots?

The word says, *he who the Son sets free is free indeed*. Think about that oxymoron for a moment - He is our Master, yet we are free indeed. If we choose to not serve Him, we become slaves to sin. Only our great God Jehovah could think of a system like that.

This is totally opposite to the world's way of thinking. You can only serve one master. If you want to serve Jesus, you have to abandon all claims to lordship of your own life. Accepting Jesus as your Master requires you to walk by faith. This is one reason why so few people find the narrow gate to salvation.

It is not uncommon for a person to have to come to the end of his rope before he is ready to allow the Lord to take control of his life.

I can speak from experience. I was taught these things as a boy, but I had to come to the end of myself as a young adult before I was ready to accept Jesus as my Lord and Savior. Since that time I have never looked back, and I can honestly say I have been abundantly blessed by surrendering totally to Him. I am convinced that you will be too.

The wages of sin always has been and always will be - death. Wages is just another word for your paycheck. Jesus declared that a worker is worthy of his paycheck. If you work for money, you get paid money. When you commit sin, you are working for your master, and your master will pay you for your work, but it's not a paycheck you want to receive. The paycheck for sin is death.

Our God offers a different and much more appealing deal. He doesn't require you to work for your salvation. In fact, He won't even *let* you work for your salvation. While the wages of sin is death, the free gift of God is eternal life!

Jesus substituted His sinless life for our sinful life. The wages of sin had to be paid, and Jesus paid it all, for all of us. The writer of the letter to the Hebrews declares that we are made holy by the shed blood of Jesus Christ. And not only are we made holy, but we are given access into heaven's most holy place.

If Jesus were the Godfather (instead of being One with God the Father), He might say, "This is an offer you cannot refuse!" Life instead of death! His blood covering our sins! Access into the very throne room of heaven!

And all we have to do is accept His free gift. The good news, the Gospel, is this: if we confess our sins, He is faithful and just to forgive us of our sins and to cleanse us from all unrighteousness.

It might sound too good to be true, too easy. "What's the catch?" A lot of people simply won't accept it as a free gift and try to find another path to God. But no other path exists.

St. Luke tells us in Acts 4:12 that, *"There is salvation in no other."* The writer of the letter to the Hebrews tells us that Jesus is our High Priest, the only one who is able to stand between sinful man and Holy God. He has spanned that gulf once and for all, and he serves eternally as our intercessor, always praying for us.

As the light of the world, Jesus came to destroy the works of darkness. As the Word of God, He came to reveal the truth of the kingdom of God, which is life and it more abundantly.

Before the foundation of the world it was God's plan to send His own Son from Heaven and ransom back mankind to Himself. The work of the cross was a complete work of redemption of whosoever will call upon the name of the Lord.

In his first letter, the Beloved Disciple, John, called Jesus "our hope." Hope is the confident expectation that something good is going to happen. He is an ever present help in time of trouble.

That doesn't mean you won't experience hard times or times of sorrow. We still live in a fallen world. I have had sorrow in my own life and I know many other followers of Jesus Christ who have experienced hard times. I cannot even imagine how you survive without knowing the God of hope. He is the only one that can restore our lives after they have been shattered.

Finally, Jesus is our coming King. After His resurrection, Jesus told His disciples He had to go away, but that He would not leave them lonely. In fact, He said, it was far better for Him to go away, because by doing so, He would send them another helper, the Holy Spirit. The Holy Spirit would empower them, teach them all things and recall to their minds all the words Jesus had taught them.

Nourishment for the Journey

Matthew 28:19 - *Go ye therefore, and make disciples of all the nations, baptizing them into the name of the Father and of the Son and of the Holy Spirit:*

Matthew 16:16 - *And Simon Peter answered and said, Thou art the Christ, the Son of the living God.*

Matthew 8:29 - *And behold, they cried out, saying, What have we to do with thee, thou Son of God? Art thou come hither to torment us before the time?*

Mark 11:23 - *Verily I say unto you, Whosoever shall say unto this mountain, Be thou taken up and cast into the sea; and shall not doubt in his heart, but shall believe that what he saith cometh to pass; he shall have it.*

Matthew 27:54 - *Now the centurion, and they that were with him watching Jesus, when they saw the earthquake, and the things that were done, feared exceedingly, saying, Truly this was the Son of God.*

Luke 1:31-33 - *And behold, thou shalt conceive in thy womb, and bring forth a son, and shalt call his name JESUS. He shall be great, and shall be called the Son of the Most High: and the Lord God shall give unto him the throne of his father David: and he shall reign over the house of Jacob for ever; and of his kingdom there shall be no end.*

John 1:33-34 - *And I knew him not: but he that sent me to baptize in water, he said unto me, Upon whomsoever thou shalt see the Spirit descending, and abiding upon him, the same is he that baptizeth in the*

Holy Spirit. And I have seen, and have borne witness that this is the Son of God.

John 11:3-5 - *The sisters therefore sent unto him, saying, Lord, behold, he whom thou lovest is sick. But when Jesus heard it, he said, This sickness is not unto death, but for the glory of God, that the Son of God may be glorified thereby. Now Jesus loved Martha, and her sister, and Lazarus.*

Luke 22:69-71 - *But from henceforth shall the Son of man be seated at the right hand of the power of God. And they all said, Art thou then the Son of God? And he said unto them, Ye say that I am. And they said, What further need have we of witness? for we ourselves have heard from his own mouth.*

Acts 9:19-21 - *And he took food and was strengthened. And he was certain days with the disciples that were at Damascus. And straightway in the synagogues he proclaimed Jesus, that he is the Son of God. And all that heard him were amazed, and said, Is not this he that in Jerusalem made havoc of them that called on this name? And he had come hither for this intent, that he might bring them bound before the chief priests.*

Luke 2:11 - *For there is born to you this day in the city of David a Saviour, who is Christ the Lord.*

Luke 4:41 - *And demons also came out from many, crying out, and saying, Thou art the Son of God. And rebuking them, he suffered them not to speak, because they knew that he was the Christ.*

John 20:30-31 - *Many other signs therefore did Jesus in the presence of the disciples, which are not written in this book: but these are written, that ye may believe that Jesus is the Christ, the Son of God; and that believing ye may have life in his name.*

John 1:29 - *On the morrow he seeth Jesus coming unto him, and saith, Behold, the Lamb of God, that taketh away the sin of the world!*

John 1:1-14 - *In the beginning was the Word, and the Word was with God, and the Word was God. The same was in the beginning with God. All things were made through him; and without him was not anything made that hath been made. In him was life; and the life was the light of men. And the light shineth in the darkness; and the darkness apprehended it not. There came a man, sent from God, whose name was John. The same came for witness, that he might bear witness of the light, that all might believe through him. He was not the light, but came that he might bear witness of the light. There was the true light, even the light which lighteth every man, coming into the world. He was in the world, and the world was made through him, and the world knew him not. He came unto his own, and they that were his own received him not. But as many as received him, to them gave he the right to become children of God, even to them that believe on his name: who were born, not of blood, nor of the will of the flesh, nor of the will of man, but of God. And the Word became flesh, and dwelt among us (and we beheld his glory, glory as of the only begotten from the Father), full of grace and truth.*

Colossians 3:16 - *Let the word of Christ dwell in you richly; in all wisdom teaching and admonishing one another with psalms and hymns and spiritual songs, singing with grace in your hearts unto God.*

John 14:6 - *Jesus saith unto him, I am the way, and the truth, and the life: no one cometh unto the Father, but by me.*

Hebrews 11:3 - *By faith we understand that the worlds have been framed by the word of God, so that what is seen hath not been made out of things which appear.*

II Peter 3:5 - *For this they willfully forget, that there were heavens from of old, and an earth compacted out of water and amidst water, by the word of God.*

Acts 10-38 - *Even Jesus of Nazareth, how God anointed him with the Holy Spirit and with power: who went about doing good, and healing all that were oppressed of the devil; for God was with him.*

Philippians 2:9-11 - *Wherefore also God highly exalted him, and gave unto him the name which is above every name; that in the name of Jesus every knee should bow, of things in heaven and things on earth and things under the earth, and that every tongue should confess that Jesus Christ is Lord, to the glory of God the Father.*

Romans 10:9-10 - *Because if thou shalt confess with thy mouth Jesus as Lord, and shalt believe in thy heart that God raised him from the dead, thou shalt be saved: for with the heart man believeth unto* *righteousness; and with the mouth confession is made unto salvation.*

Titus 2:11 - *For the grace of God hath appeared, bringing salvation to all men.*

Ephesians 1:7 - *In whom we have our redemption through his blood, the forgiveness of our trespasses, according to the riches of his grace.*

Colossians 1:14 - *In whom we have our redemption, the forgiveness of our sins.*

Hebrews 9:22 - *And according to the law, I may almost say, all things are cleansed with blood, and apart from shedding of blood there is no remission.*

Proverbs 12:1 - *Whoso loveth correction loveth knowledge; But he that hateth reproof is brutish.*

Romans 6:23 - *For the wages of sin is death; but the free gift of God is eternal life in Christ Jesus our Lord.*

Hebrews 10:9-10, 19-20 - *Then hath he said, Lo, I am come to do thy will. He taketh away the first, that he may establish the second. By which will we have been sanctified through the offering of the body of Jesus Christ once for all. Having therefore, brethren, boldness to enter into the holy place by the blood of Jesus, by the way which he dedicated for us, a new and living way, through the veil, that is to say, his flesh.*

I John 1:9 - *If we confess our sins, he is faithful and righteous to forgive us our sins, and to cleanse us from all unrighteousness.*

Acts 4:12 - *And in none other is there salvation: for neither is there any other name under heaven, that is given among men, wherein we must be saved.*

Hebrews 8:1 - *Now in the things which we are saying the chief point is this: We have such a high priest, who sat down on the right hand of the throne of the Majesty in the heavens.*

Hebrews 7:25 - *Wherefore also he is able to save to the uttermost them that draw near unto God through him, seeing he ever liveth to make intercession for them.*

John 8:12 - *Again therefore Jesus spake unto them, saying, I am the light of the world: he that followeth me shall not walk in the darkness, but shall have the light of life.*

John 10:10 - *The thief cometh not, but that he may steal, and kill, and destroy: I came that they may have life, and may have it abundantly.*

I John 1:1 - *That which was from the beginning, that which we have heard, that which we have seen with our eyes, that which we beheld, and our hands handled, concerning the Word of life.*

Psalm 121:1-2 - *I will lift up mine eyes unto the mountains: From whence shall my help come? My help cometh from Jehovah, Who made heaven and earth.*

John 14:16-26 - *And I will pray the Father, and he shall give you another Comforter, that he may be with you for ever, even the Spirit of truth: whom the world cannot receive; for it beholdeth him not, neither knoweth him: ye know him; for he abideth with you,* *and shall be in you. I will not leave you desolate: I come unto you. Yet a little while, and the world beholdeth me no more; but ye behold me: because I live, ye shall live also. In that day ye shall know that I am in my Father, and ye in me, and I in you. He that hath my commandments, and keepeth them, he it is that loveth me: and he that loveth me shall be loved of my Father, and I will love him, and will manifest myself unto him. Judas (not Iscariot) saith unto him, Lord, what is come to pass that thou wilt manifest thyself unto us, and not unto the world? Jesus answered and said unto him, If a man love me, he will keep my word: and my Father will love him, and we will come unto him, and make our abode with him. He that loveth me not keepeth not my words: and the word which ye hear is not mine, but the Father's who sent me. These things have I spoken unto you, while yet abiding with you. But the Comforter, even the Holy Spirit, whom the Father will send in my name, he shall teach you all things, and bring to your remembrance all that I said unto you.*

John 16:7 - *Nevertheless I tell you the truth: It is expedient for you that I go away; for if I go not away, the Comforter will not come unto you; but if I go, I will send him unto you.*

Chapter 7
Embracing The Person Of The Holy Spirit

The third person of the Godhead (commonly referred to theologically as the Holy Trinity) is the Holy Spirit.

There has been a lot of confusion both inside and outside the church about just who the Holy Spirit is. While there is much more to the Holy Spirit than you or I could ever hope to fathom, there is much that the Scriptures tells us about this important member of the Holy Trinity.

The Holy Spirit is the visible and invisible force of God in the earth. The Holy Spirit was present at the very beginning of creation. According to the Genesis account, He is the movement or agent of force that emanates from God's throne.

The Holy Spirit is like the breath of God that proceeds from His mouth when He speaks the Word. Every time God speaks, His word is performed by the breath behind the words. In the Old Testament, God said, *"Let there be light, and there was light!"* A New Testament example would be Jesus at the tomb of Lazarus. Jesus, prayed to His Father, then spoke the words, *"Lazarus, come forth!"* The breath, or Spirit, behind the word produced life in the lifeless body of the dead man.

Many of us are familiar with the famous Sunday school story about Jesus calming the storm. If you didn't have the benefit of attending Sunday school as a child, the story goes something like this: Jesus was in a boat on the sea with his disciples when a big storm came up. Things got so bad, the disciples (including some seasoned sailors) were afraid the boat would sink. Jesus apparently wasn't too worried about it, because he was up in the front of the boat, fast asleep. The disciples woke Jesus up. He stood up and rebuked the wind, and the sea immediately calmed down. He spoke to the wind and the Wind or Breath of His Words (that is the Holy Spirit) took authority over the wind and storm.

Jesus spoke with authority to demons, commanding them to leave their hosts, and the force behind His words were as powerful as dynamite. Speaking to a mountain and commanding it to move might seem impossible - and it is in the natural. Isn't it great to know that we serve a God who is supernatural!

Jesus recognized that we would need the person and work of the Holy Spirit in our lives, and He spent a lot of time talking about it to His disciples. He told them in the Gospel according to John that He would send them a helper, a comforter, the Holy Spirit, who would bring to their remembrance all of His words.

Jesus knew He couldn't stay with His disciples forever. And even in His glorified, resurrected body, He couldn't be everywhere at once. Since He was about to leave the earth and ascend to the right hand of His Father, He took the time to tell His disciples to wait for the anointing of the Holy Spirit that He was sending to them before they embarked on their ministry.

Why did they need this Holy Spirit then, and why do we need the Holy Spirit now? Because He is the wind, *the power*, to produce the life of God in us. He is the breath of God in the world. As He was with Jesus, so shall He be with us.

We are commanded in the Scriptures to be holy, because God is holy. I've heard countless sermons talking about how we, as believers, should live holy lives, abstaining from sin. Well, that's a great idea. Those of us who have been born again desire to do right, but we are at war with our old nature. The fact is, we simply can't do it on our own. We are too weak in our flesh. As the Apostle Paul tells us, all have sinned and fallen short of the glory of God.

Thankfully, what we cannot accomplish in our own strength, we can accomplish through the Holy Spirit, who has been given to us to overcome the world. The heart of God dwells in our spirit when we accept Christ, but the fullness of His great glory and power must be drawn on daily.

When I enter a dark room, I turn the light on so I can see. The light doesn't come on of its own accord. I flip the switch, and the light bulb draws on an external power source allowing it to illuminate the room. The same principal applies between us and the Holy Spirit. The power to overcome sin and to accomplish the things God has called us to do is available through the Holy Spirit, but it requires us to daily tap into that power source.

The Gospel of St. Luke reveals just how important the presence of the Holy Spirit is in the life of every believer. John the Baptizer was baptizing people for the remission of their sins. Although Jesus had committed no sin, He submitted Himself to John's baptism in order to fulfill all righteousness. When He came up out of the water, the Holy Spirit descended upon Him.

He would need the power of the Holy Spirit in the days ahead, for immediately after His baptism, the Holy Spirit led Jesus into the wilderness where He was tempted by the devil for 40 days. Through the indwelling power of the Holy Spirit, Jesus overcame those temptations in the wilderness. He then returned in the fullness and power of the Holy Spirit, and went about doing good works.

You might have seen that old bumper sticker that read "God is my co-pilot." It's a sweet, though theologically unsound, idea: *I'm not in this by myself; I am not walking this path alone; I am getting help from God; God is helping to steer my life.* The problem is a co-pilot is not in charge. God doesn't want to just be along for my ride to help out.

God is the One who designed the ship. He's the one who built the ship. He's the one who created the currents the ship rides on. Wouldn't it make more sense to make God the pilot, and you and I ride in the shotgun seat as the co-pilot? Let Him steer the ship and we go along with Him. This was His idea with sending the Holy Spirit.

A few years ago the world witnessed a near disaster averted because of the expert work of the master pilot. An airliner filled with passengers couldn't reach the runway at the airport, and had to make an emergency landing on the Hudson River. The pilot made an in-flight course correction based on the information he was given. The seasoned veteran pilot determined the best and safest course of action was to set the plane down in the Hudson River. He calmly and competently brought the plane and its passengers safely down on the river.

Sometimes your life is a disaster waiting to happen. If you have the controls, chances are when those times come, you will crash and burn. Having a master pilot at the controls of your life makes a lot more sense, don't you think. Jesus is the master pilot of life. He can bring you safely through any storm.

As a master pilot, Jesus gave us an example of how to navigate the path of life. Amazingly, the Master Pilot Jesus did not steer His own ship! Instead, He only did what He saw the Father do, and He only spoke what He heard the Father saying.

If our Lord relied totally on His Father for His agenda, doesn't it seem right for us to do the same?

I've served the Lord Jesus for more than 40 years, and during that time I've discovered that when I let the Holy Spirit lead me, I am successful. When I try to lead by myself apart from the Holy Spirit, the results are a crap shoot at best. Decisions I've made without prayer and listening to the Holy Spirit usually either get me in trouble or have less than successful conclusions.

During our child-rearing years, Patti and I discovered what seems to be a universal truth of parenthood: Children struggle to do their chores right the first time. While your children might be perfect, ours would almost always try to take a short cut, and inevitably make a mistake and have to redo the project.

Unfortunately, this trait isn't limited to children. Mankind as a whole always seems to want to take the easy way out. Such shortcuts always fail, and the job requires a do-over. I don't know about you, but I really dislike having to do something twice to get the job done right.

One of those truism we all learned in school is, *the shortest distance between two points is a straight line*. This is as true in life as it is in geometry. The straight and narrow path requires less effort, costs less to take, and quite frankly is the only road that will get you to the finish line.

But the straight path in the Spirit doesn't always look straight to our natural eyes. That's one more reason we need the indwelling power of the Holy Spirit in our lives. As the prophet Isaiah declared, *"Your ears will hear a word behind you, This is the way, walk in it, whenever you turn to the right or to the left."*

I love my GPS. When traveling to someplace new, I don't have to guess at the best route. My GPS already knows the way and it has the route figured out before I even get started. The Holy Spirit is our spiritual GPS. My friend the Holy Spirit knows the correct route for the day before you even get out of bed. All we have to do is hook up with Him. The Holy Spirit speaks to us, telling us which directions to take and which routes to avoid.

We need the Holy Spirit to direct our paths, and to empower us to overcome the temptations of this world.

Nourishment for the Journey

Genesis 1:2 - *And the earth was waste and void; and darkness was upon the face of the deep: and the Spirit of God moved upon the face of the waters.*

John 14:16 - *And I will pray the Father, and he shall give you another Comforter, that he may be with you for ever.*

Luke 4:1 - *And Jesus, full of the Holy Spirit, returned from the Jordan, and was led in the Spirit in the wilderness.*

John 5:19,30 - *Jesus therefore answered and said unto them, Verily, verily, I say unto you, The Son can do nothing of himself, but what he seeth the Father doing: for what things soever he doeth, these the Son also doeth in like manner...I can of myself do nothing: as I hear, I judge: and my judgment is righteous; because I seek not mine own will, but the will of him that sent me.*

Chapter 8
The Holy Spirit Is Truth

In this chapter we will take a look at the power and purpose of the Holy Spirit in our lives. Jesus said, *I am the way, the truth and the life*. He sent the Holy Spirit to guide us into all truth. Since Jesus is the truth, the primary function of the Holy Spirit is to lead us to Jesus.

The Beloved Disciple, John, tells us that the Spirit of truth testifies about Jesus and keeps us from stumbling over false doctrine. He will guide us, just as He guided Jesus in His earthly walk. How awesome is that! The Lord of Lords and King of Kings has given to us the connection to the Father's wisdom and knowledge. We don't have to guess at what makes life work. The Giver of life and the Creator of the universe is willing to impart at any moment what we need to know by His breath, His Holy Spirit, in us.

The Old Testament book of Proverbs tells us that the spirit of man is the candle of the Lord that searches the innermost being. You've probably heard the ladies talking about their "women's intuition" or the guys talking about having a "gut feeling." This is actually the Spirit of the Lord touching the seat of our emotions and trying to get a message to us.

When you feel that stirring in your spirit, you might need to do a little soul searching to make sure it's coming from the Holy Spirit. You might need to mull this thing over until the peace that passes understanding comes over you.

Peace is a great indicator of the presence of the Holy Spirit in any situation. In his letter to the Colossians, Paul encourages believers to *let the peace of God rule in your hearts*, and to *let the word of Christ dwell in you richly in all wisdom; teaching and admonishing one another in psalms and hymns and spiritual songs, singing with grace in your hearts to the Lord*. Man! This verse is full of goodies.

Let the word of Christ dwell in you richly. It's worth repeating. Not religiously, or loosely, but *richly*.

The Word of God is Spirit and that Word connects to our spirits, convicting (convincing) us of our wrong thoughts and actions. Without the Word and the Holy Spirit there would be no difference between us or those outside of Christ.

The Holy Spirit keeps us from stumbling. He shows us the truth about our own wickedness and offenses we commit against the throne of God. We need this Truth-Teller in us to effect the change toward godliness that the Father had in mind for us all along.

God is good and His purposes toward us are for life and life more abundantly. The problem is, we don't know what abundant life looks like. It takes God to show that to us, to reveal it to us. He sends His Holy Breath - His Holy Spirit - to speak to our innermost being, our hearts.

It is through this convicting, convincing power of the Holy Spirit that we repent, have remorse and connect with the truth being revealed in the depths of hearts. It sounds awful, but it is a good thing to discover how wretched we are. If you don't know you have a cancer that is eating away at your body, you'll never seek treatment. The Holy Spirit serves to diagnose our sin. Once we see ourselves for what we really are, He can purge us clean.

Let Christ dwell in you richly in all wisdom.

When I was a young man sometimes I would hear a much older person say, *you seem wise beyond your years.* How did that happen? It was His wisdom revealed to my heart that came out of my mouth. There have been times I was preaching and things came out of my mouth that I never intended to say. I'd stop and think, *Wait a moment; what did I just say? That was really good and it is not in my notes. It is hot off the press.*

Some might say it is the anointing at that moment, and I would agree with that. Our commission is to do our best to stay in the flow of His anointing at every moment.

Jesus was never distracted. He stayed in the flow continually, and He declared we would do the same works He did. That means we can continually stay in the flow of the anointing too. I have not acquired that yet, but I'm not discouraged. I'm encouraged because the same power that raised Christ from the dead dwells in me, and you, richly.

Nourishment for the Journey

John 16:13 - *Howbeit when he, the Spirit of truth, is come, he shall guide you into all the truth: for he shall not speak from himself; but what things soever he shall hear, these shall he speak: and he shall declare unto you the things that are to come.*

John 15:26 - *But when the Comforter is come, whom I will send unto you from the Father, even the Spirit of truth, which proceedeth from the Father, he shall bear witness of me.*

John 16:1 - *These things have I spoken unto you, that ye should not be caused to stumble.*

Proverbs 20:27 - *The spirit of man is the lamp of Jehovah, Searching all his innermost parts.*

Colossians 3:15-16 - *And let the peace of Christ rule in your hearts, to the which also ye were called in one body; and be ye thankful. Let the word of Christ dwell in you richly; in all wisdom teaching and admonishing one another with psalms and hymns and spiritual songs, singing with grace in your hearts unto God.*

Chapter 9
The Holy Spirit Is Power

B*ut ye shall receive power, after that the Holy Ghost is come upon you; and ye shall be witnesses unto me both in Jerusalem and all Judea and Samaria and unto the uttermost parts of the earth.* (Acts 1:8 KJV)

We always think of a person's last words as being important; of being worthy of being preserved. These were Jesus' last words to the disciples before He departed out of their midst into Heaven.

He was informing them of a great event that was about to take place in their lives. They were about to be empowered by the Holy Spirit - an event which would transform them into bold and confident witnesses, giving them the power to go forth into His ministry.

Just prior to saying these words, Jesus instructed His disciples to go back to Jerusalem and wait until the promise of the Father came. *John baptized with water*, He said, *but I will baptize you with the Holy Spirit, and His power.*

If those disciples, who walked with Jesus for three years and heard His teaching first-hand, needed a power greater than themselves to transform them into bold, confident witnesses, what makes us think we can do it without that same power?

We cannot.

One of the Greek words that we translate into the English word, *power,* is e*xousia. Exousia* is delegated power. It means you have authority, jurisdiction or influence delegated to you from a higher source. The disciples performed the same kinds of powerful acts as Jesus - casting out demons, healing the sick, performing miracles - through the *exousia*, the authority delegated to them from God through the Holy Spirit working in them.

I have personally witnessed on numerous occasions the *exousia*, the delegated power and authority of the Holy Spirit, opening blind eyes, making deaf people hear, casting out demons and even raising the dead!

"How can these things happen?" you might wonder.

God has not stopped being God. Jesus has not stopped being Lord of lords. The Holy Spirit didn't stop being active in the lives of Christ's disciples. God - the Father, Son and Holy Spirit - is the same yesterday, today and forever. The Word tells us that at the mention of His name every knee on earth shall bow. Last time I looked, we were still on earth. Why shouldn't the knees of cancer, depression and evil bow before the name of Jesus Christ?

Sometimes we try to dumb down the person and work of the Holy Spirit. We don't understand how the wind blows, and we don't understand how the Holy Spirit works; and sometimes we just don't like that. I even know of some groups who refuse to accept and teach that the New Testament book of the Acts of the Apostles is valid for the church today.

I believe it all boils down to surrender. The real reason for not going there is, it requires you to give up the lordship of your life. Perhaps you're afraid of looking foolish to the world. But friendship with the world is enmity with God, and only leads to death. The gospel is power, and it is life abundant!

Forget how you look to the world. Think instead about how you look to the Father. He sent His only Son into this world to save you and me, to give us complete salvation. Surrender your pride, humble yourself under the mighty hand of God and He will exalt you.

It sounds simple enough, but don't get the idea that it's easy. If you give God total control of your life He may ask you to do something you won't like, or that you think might embarrass you.

But stop and think about that mentality for just a moment. If you have children, you've probably asked them to do a chore they didn't want to do, or chances are you've heard them say something like, "Dad, please don't embarrass me when my friends come over. Maybe you could take Mom on a date, and not even be here."

That kind of whining over chores and so-called embarrassing situations comes with the teenage territory, but it is no way for mature adults to behave. God has never asked me to do anything that didn't result in my ultimate good, and He has never embarrassed me. Instead, He has graciously allowed me to be a witness for Him, and to witness His great power.

If we only accept part of God's baptism, just the *Father* part, or just the *Son* part, and leave off the *Holy Spirit* part, we are not whole. We are incomplete in our faith and in our walk with God.

I've met so many believers who are struggling, I mean really struggling. When I ask them if the Holy Spirit is in control of their lives, they just don't want to go there. It seems like some folks would rather endure the struggles of life on their own than surrender to the gentle wooing of the Holy Spirit.

It's a bit like when we go to the beach. My wife beckons me to "Come on in, the water's fine!" But I just wave from the shore. "No thanks," I say. "I'm fine up here on the shore."

She keeps beckoning for a while, then finally gives up and plays around in the water, having a great time. I watch for a while, seeing how much she is enjoying herself, and when I can't take it any more I take off running and jump in. Once I'm all wet I discover how wonderful it feels. It's refreshing, relaxing and fun. I don't ever want to get out.

It is the same when you experience the fullness of the Holy Spirit. When you receive Him and fully plunge into Him, you will find He is refreshing, relaxing and fun. You can do that right now. Jesus said He would liberally give the Holy Spirit to those who ask.

Come on in, my friend. The water's fine!

Nourishment for the Journey

Acts 1:8 - *But ye shall receive power, when the Holy Spirit is come upon you: and ye shall be my witnesses both in Jerusalem, and in all Judaea and Samaria, and unto the uttermost part of the earth.*

Hebrews 13:8 - *Jesus Christ is the same yesterday and today, yea and forever.*

James 4:10 - *Humble yourselves in the sight of the Lord, and he shall exalt you.*

Chapter 10
Concerning Spiritual Gifts

The Apostle Paul wrote to the Corinthian church, *Now concerning the gifts of the Spirit brethren I do not want you to be ignorant, or uniformed.* In other words, it is vitally important for you to know the working of the Holy Spirit, brothers and sisters. This is an essential ingredient for your success as a follower of Christ.

Paul goes on to explain that even though there are different gifts of the Spirit, it is the same Spirit who distributes these gifts, and He disburses these gifts to each believer to be used for the common good of the whole body of believers.

When the Holy Spirit is welcomed by us, when He indwells us and has absolute control in our lives He is able to use these great gifts in and through us, for not just our own benefit but for the edification of those that are around us.

The Holy Spirit imparts the gift of supernatural wisdom - an understanding we did not learn, but just instantly comes to us. My wife calls it the MacGyver gift. Remember that old television show? The hero, MacGyver, would be in an impossible situation with no solution and no way out. But somehow, he would get a sudden burst of inspiration. He'd look around find something to fashion just the right tool to use to make his escape.

Of course MacGyver was just a cleverly written TV show. But the truth is, the Holy Spirit can provide just that kind of inspiration. He gives us supernatural answers to problems around us that we could never come up with on our own.

Time after time the Holy Spirit has given me supernatural understanding of ways to fix problems I had no training to do. When I built our first house, the only house I had ever built was a birdhouse. I knew how to use building tools, like a hammer, saw tape measure, but building a house isn't the same as making a bird house. It requires skills, knowledge and experience that I simply did not have.

When I was asleep at night I often had dreams of how to build the house, step-by-step, for the next day. These dreams went on each time I hit a snag until the house was finished. That was the Holy Spirit giving me the understanding to build something I had no formal training in.

I believe most of our inventions came from people with some form of this gift working in them, even if they did not know that's what was going on.

Knowledge is important, but knowledge by itself isn't very useful. Wisdom is the ability to grasp a situation and react properly to it. Natural wisdom, what we used to call *common sense*, involves knowledge and experience - learning how things work over a period of time through testing and trials and arriving at specific conclusions. Supernatural wisdom as a gift from the Holy Spirit bypasses the learning and experience required by nature. The Holy Spirit already knows all things. He knows how the natural order works, so He can impart that wisdom instantly, making us look like a bunch of little MacGyver's.

Relying on the Holy Spirit makes us wise beyond our years. He councils us by the Word of truth, the Bible, and by the interpretation of what is going on around us. Where we see only a tiny part of what is going on around us in both the natural and the spiritual realms, He sees the big picture and can impart to us instantly the answer to every problem that confronts us. Having the supernatural gift of wisdom from the Holy Spirit is like holding the owner's manual for life.

Of course you could just try to obtain wisdom through life experience. But experience is a harsh teacher; it gives you the test first and then teaches you the lesson. Why go through all that testing and heartache when you can ask the Author of the book?

This is not to imply you don't need to study to learn how things work. The Apostle Paul encouraged believers to study to show yourself approved, a workman who doesn't need to be ashamed of the quality of his work.

But the Holy Spirit distributes His gifts as He sees fit for the common good. Someone around you may have that instant insight, that remedy you need from the Holy Spirit. That is the wisdom from the Holy Spirit. The Holy Spirit was given to us to be our helper. Let Him help.

Another gift of the he Holy Spirit is supernatural knowledge; things that we could not know in the natural, but that are important for our own spiritual growth, or for another person.

An example of the gift of knowledge occurred while we were having our mid-week home study with our new church-plant group. As we were praying I saw in my spirit a wagon being pulled and it was full of gifts needing to be unwrapped. I shared that word of knowledge with the group.

In our midst was a new lady I had not met before. She began to laugh out loud.

"I am Miss Wagoner," she said. "I came to this meeting to find out about the gifts of the Holy Spirit."

The Holy Spirit gave me the gift of a word of knowledge, and he used that gift for the common good of the group. That word was a confirmation to Miss Wagoner that she was supposed to be at that meeting. God, by the Spirit, had what she needed and connected her with it.

On another occasion as my wife and I were about to leave after church, an elder stopped me. A woman said she knew I was an evangelist and wanted me to pray with her at the front of the church. I could see she was in great pain, both physically and emotionally. The Holy Spirit spoke to me.

"Who is Sally?" I asked.

She was stunned. "Sally is my sister," she replied.

I did not know this woman. I had never seen her before. But the Holy Spirit knew her and told me her sister's name. It certainly got her attention.

"Why do you hate your sister?" I asked, again drawing on knowledge from the Holy Spirit.

"I don't hate my sister," she insisted.

"Tell me about your sister," I said.

"Well, my sister was born on Father's Day," she began.

"You don't have to tell me anymore," I said. "When your sister was born on Father's Day, your father said, *What a wonderful gift for me on Father's day*! From that time on, you thought your father loved your sister more than he loved you. But he never thought that. You imagined it and held it in your heart all these years. It has manifested into this sickness you have now."

She began to weep uncontrollably.

"Just let it out," I told her. "Here is what you need to do to get well. First, forgive your sister, right now - even though she had nothing to do with being born on Father's Day. Second, forgive your father for saying what he said - even though he was not implying that your sister was more special than you. Third, forgive your Heavenly Father - because He is the one that chose the day of your sister's birth, and He had a good reason for it."

She forgave all three and instantly her countenance changed. You could see peace settle all about her. Her twisted face and life were gone.

I have seen the Holy Spirit do this kind of thing many times, not just through me but through others as well. If you've ever watched the 700 Club on TV you might recall seeing the host and co-host calling out sicknesses and problems that people watching were experiencing. This is a great gift and it is available to you through the Holy Spirit for the common good of others.

Notice I keep repeating, *for the common good*. The gifts of the Holy Spirit are supernatural, but the exercise of those gifts are intended to be a common, everyday occurrence in the kingdom of God. To our Heavenly Father this is just a normal thing. It should be a normal thing for us to operate in the gifts of the Holy Spirit.

Another wonderful gift of the Holy Spirit is supernatural faith. Faith is an absolute conviction in something that makes you unmovable in confidence.

Scripture teaches us that we can grow our faith, and one way to do that is by listening to godly instruction. Faith comes by *hearing* the Word of God. Another way to increase faith is by studying the Word of God.

But the supernatural gift of faith is not something you can acquire on your own. It only comes from the Holy Spirit. When you have it, you just know that you know.

Over the years I have responded instantly to specific needs in people lives by laying hands on them, as the Word instructs. As a result, I've seen the Lord work many mighty miracles. I didn't plan those instances; they just rose up in me and I responded with a supernatural faith that there would be a miraculous end to the situation at hand.

This gift of faith is not something you can obtain through study, although studying the Word of God is a good thing, an essential thing. Jesus did not have to study to learn how to turn water into wine at the wedding feast in Cana. He didn't go to medical school to learn how to restore sight to blind Bartimaeus. He didn't study agriculture or animal husbandry before feeding thousands of people with a little boy's lunch of five loaves of bread and a couple of fish. He simply responded to the Spirit within Himself. He knew, He just knew the Father heard His words and would answer the request.

Jesus told the disciples it was imperative for Him to go away so that the Holy Spirit would come to us and be our helper in faith. He said we would do the same works that He did. How is that possible? Through the Spirit that raised Jesus from the dead, which is the same Spirit that dwells in us.

It's important to note that the Holy Spirit is not a bully. The Spirit makes gifts available to believers, but will not force those gifts on you. Our part in the equation is to fully embrace the Holy Spirit, and give over control of our lives so that He can bring all His gifts into us for the common good of all. If we surrender to the Holy Spirit, He will exalt the name of Jesus through us in the most unusual ways.

I was at a little league baseball game with my boys. One of the players got hit hard in the nose with the ball, and blood started gushing out. A crowd gathered around the kid and they rushed him over to the water fountain to wash the blood off and try to stop the flow with cold water.

I didn't think about applying ice or a cold rag to his busted nose. Instead, I just reached through the crowd and spoke to the boy's nose. I commanded it to stop bleeding in the name of Jesus, and quoted the Word of God over it. The bleeding stopped immediately.

This is an example of the supernatural gift of faith in operation. When you just know to do something that goes beyond your own faith, and you are compelled to do it by the Holy Spirit, it will work. This is the supernatural gift of faith at work. Let the gift of the Holy Spirit shine forth in those moments.

We have moved a number of times during our lives. When we made those moves it was by faith. The Holy Spirit compelled us to do so. If left up to our own reasoning, it's unlikely we would have made any of those moves. But when we knew by His Spirit that it was time to make a move, there was an unwavering faith about the situation that brought peace.

I've made other moves in my life that just looked like the right thing to do. They sounded good. They were reasonable moves. The only problem was, they weren't part of God's plan for our lives. My natural reasoning ended up leading us into the bondage of debt, just as the Hebrew children of old wound up in captivity.

When we stepped out in His supernatural faith by His Spirit we were delivered from that bondage. It was a beautiful thing. We must come to trust His working in us. It is His faith at work in us, not our wishful thinking and reasoning, which causes us to be victorious. Don't fight the urging of the Holy Spirit. Surrender to Him. Work in tandem with Him. Your response to the Spirit is vital to the common good because, believe me, someone needs what you have to offer through the Holy Spirit.

The Holy Spirit gives the gift of healings. Supernatural healing is a process; it is not an instantaneous miracle. Healing occurs as a result of the prayer of faith.

You may have a specific word of knowledge about the situation which you speak out, and the healing takes place over a period of time. I once prayed over a man who was bent over. I told him if he would roll out of bed and crawl to the window to pull himself up each day for the next seven days, that on the seventh day he would be able to stand upright. He believed the words I spoke and it came to pass just as it was told him.

The prophet Elisha told Naaman to go dip himself in the muddy Jordan River seven times, and he would be healed of leprosy. At first Naaman refused, but then obeyed the word of the Lord, spoken by the man of God. Once he obeyed, he was cleansed of his leprosy.

We could split hairs and say that maybe that instance was a miracle or maybe it was a healing. It might have been a little bit of both. He was not cleansed the first, second, third, fourth, fifth or sixth time he dipped in the Jordan, but after the seventh time, following a process. It was a short timespan, but a process none the less.

I knew a man who was in the hospital, dying from diabetes. His feet had gangrene and the doctors thought the only way to save him was to amputate the putrid appendages. We prayed over him, and the next day the doctors decided to put off the surgery for a couple of days. We prayed again, and they waited a couple of more days. By the following week his feet had completely recovered. The doctors were astounded.

"We don't understand this reversal," they told the man. "We have never seen this happen before. But one thing we do know - you will never walk again."

To their amazement, the man stood up and walked across the room.

This is how the gift of healing works.

Another example of the gift of healing involved a member of our church who constantly developed large and painful kidney stones that had to be surgically removed or treated with stone-busting sonic waves. One Sunday he came forward for prayer and told me he had one that he could not pass. I prayed and asked the Lord to turn it to powder so it would pass.

That night he passed a white cloudy substance without the pain that usually accompanies passing a kidney stone. The Lord pulverized that rock and it passed.

This was an example of supernatural healing, because he did not have a problem with kidney stones after that.

We prayed over a pastor friend who had a chronic back problem. He was healed instantly and the problem never returned. This was a combination of the miraculous and a healing. When the gift of miracles is involved there is no process; it is instantaneous. When the gift of healing happens, it fixes the problem from then on.

We have seen hearts repaired, circulatory systems fixed, eyes returned to 20/20, respiratory problems cured and cancers disappear over a matter of weeks, all due to the healing gift of the Holy Spirit.

The Holy Spirit works the miraculous. The story of the boy at the ball game was not just the gift of faith but the gift of the working of miracles. During my forty-something years of ministry, I have seen hundreds of unexplainable events take place. I have witnessed short legs grow out, blind eyes open, deaf ears hear, cancers leave, broken bones instantly joined back together, cars run on empty gas tanks and the list goes on. Beyond my own personal experience, I've heard innumerable stories from people of God whom I know to be reputable. Bottom line: our great God is the same yesterday, today and forever. He worked miracles in the time of Moses, and He worked miracles in the time of Jesus and the Apostles. He still works miracles today, and He will continue to work miracles until the day Jesus returns to claim His bride, the Church!

It is true there are some imitators out there, but to imitate means you have to have something that was real. If there are fake miraculous events, then there are real miraculous events.

Some people try to explain away the miraculous. "It was just a coincidence," they say. No, it wasn't. It was a miracle! I not only have witnessed miracles, but I have experienced them first hand.

On one occasion, a pastor in town came to see me. I was new in town, and this brother had heard that miracles and healings were happening at our church. He could not believe it, so he marched into my office and loudly proclaimed, "I came to hear from the horse's mouth that miracles take place here. "I just don't believe it's true. I want to see if this is a work of the occult!"

"You will never see a miracle," I declared to the man.

"Why not?" he demanded to know.

"Because you have to have faith, and you do not believe," I replied. "You just said so."

That man hung his head and walked out very quietly.

I cannot understand Christian groups who insist on denying the power of the Holy Spirit. Do they really believe the Holy Spirit is like a cheap battery; only good for a season and then thrown out?

The Holy Spirit is the third member of the Holy Trinity. He is the breath and wind of the Father at work in the earth!

Still, it is no wonder these groups never see the moving of the Holy Spirit in their churches. He only works when He is invited in. If He is not invited, He will not show up!

The Apostle Paul tells the church to not quench the Holy Spirit. The Spirit of God is like a consuming fire, yet Paul is saying there is something you can do to quench or put out the fire of the Holy Spirit. But it doesn't sound like a good idea to me.

The Holy Spirit is our source of godly power. He enables us to walk in authority over sickness, disease and demons. His power working through us can effect miracles. Why in the world would you even want to be a Christian if it does not afford you the power to change?

The word *Christ* means *the Anointed One*. To be a Christian means to be *a little Christ* or *a little anointed one*. The anointing refers to being covered by and filled with the Holy Spirit, the Breath and Wind of God.

Jesus, the Christ, sent us the Holy Spirit to enable us to walk like He walked, talk like He talked, and do the works that He did. I am concerned with groups that don't get that.

When I came to Christ, I wasn't looking for a church or religion; I was looking for a Savior. I didn't need a bunch of rules and regulations. I needed an all powerful God, one who was powerful enough to deliver me from all my lost-ness. I was looking for a champion, one who could conquer my enemies.

I found this savior in the person of Jesus Christ. I found Him to be compassionate and loving, and yes, powerful enough to keep me all the days of life. I love Him, because of His great love, demonstrated to me by the gifts of His Holy Spirit.

Another gift of the Holy Spirit is prophecy. There has been some confusion about this gift of the Spirit. Some people think of prophecy as fortune-telling, and nothing could be further from the truth. Prophecy is the act of speaking the Word of God, and it can be either *foretelling* or *forth-telling*.

The great prophets of old often proved they were speaking from God by *foretelling* of coming events. At other times they prophesied by *forth-telling*, by speaking strong words of course correction for Israel.

Jesus told the disciples that the Holy Spirit would convict or reprove the world of sin. One of the primary jobs of a prophet under the anointing of the Holy Spirit is to bring forth correction to the body of Christ. The Apostle Paul was exercising the gift of prophecy when he spoke correction to the early believers. He was *forth-telling*, or *exhorting,* the body of Christ to be more like Christ.

Spiritual leaders today who hear strong words from the Spirit, and send those messages forth to the body of Christ, exhorting us to turn from our transgressions against the kingdom of God and live more Christ-like lives, are exercising the gift of prophecy.

Like all the gifts of the Spirit, prophecy is intended for the common good of the body. But it is also an outward gift for nations, as the prophet issues the call to repentance. Righteousness exalts a nation, but sin is a reproach to any people. We have a tendency to forget that we are to seek first the Kingdom of God and His righteousness. God uses prophecy to awaken His people, to bring us back to center in the Kingdom of God.

In the old days, prophets were sometimes referred to as *seers*. They would see something in the Spirit and forth-tell it to the congregation of Israel. This is still a valid work of the Holy Spirit in the Church today. Some individuals have a special anointing to serve in the office of the prophet, but the Holy Spirit can choose to use any believer who is filled with the Spirit to prophecy about things they see in the spirit realm.

Don't get the idea that this is spooky, or some kind of spiritual mumbo jumbo. The Scriptures tell us that the Spirit makes intercession for us, because He knows what we need even when we don't. It should be a comfort to know that the Holy Spirit can communicate the direction and will of the Father to us and through us for the common good of His body.

When the Holy Spirit moves through the gift of prophecy, it is always done decently and in-order. If you're in a service when prophecy is indecent or out of order, you can bet the Holy Spirit is not involved.

Prophecy is always about revealing the Word of God, and sometimes that means foretelling future events. A number of Biblical books, both Old and New Testament, are filled with prophecy regarding future events, including the books of Daniel, Ezekiel, Isaiah and Revelation. God still shows His people things that will come to pass at some future time by the prophetic gift of the Holy Spirit.

Another valuable gift of the Holy Spirit is the gift of discerning what is going on in the spirit realm. Sometimes, because we live in the physical realm, we forget that there is another realm that is usually hidden from our view; the invisible, spiritual realm where all kinds of stuff is going on all the time. If you've ever encountered a demon-possessed person you know what I am talking about.

Here's a thought: if people can be possessed by demonic spirits, can't they be led by the Holy Spirit? You have the option to be filled with His presence as much as you want, by giving control of your life over to Him. But unlike demonic spirits who mean to do you harm, the Holy Spirit will never overpower your free will. He is a Helper and a Comforter, sometimes referred to as the Paraclete - *the one who comes along side*.

Since the Holy Spirit knows all things from the beginning to their end, He sees things before they happen. How awesome! He gives us discernment about spiritual implications of situations that swirl around us. This doesn't always have to do with demonic influences. Sometimes the Holy Spirit gives us discernment about things that relate to our lives and our flesh. When you have the option of taking two different paths to arrive at the same destination, He can provide supernatural discernment that might help you avoid a bad wreck, or perhaps set you on the path to encounter that wreck so you can help the people involved.

You might get a 'check in your spirit' about going into a certain part of town, or about going into debt with that new car. The Holy Spirit might give you discernment about what to look at, what to eat or what to drink.

We can't look into another person's heart and judge their motives, but the Holy Spirit can. And He can give you discernment to prevent you from forming alliances with certain people. He can guard your hearts from getting involved with the wrong crowd. It's like having a personal bodyguard for your body, soul, mind and spirit.

The Holy Spirit offers us the gift of speaking with other tongues. This is a controversial gift of the Spirit in the minds of a number of contemporary denominations, who seem to believe this particular gift somehow faded away when the original apostles died. They believe tongues was a phenomenon used by the Holy Spirit to validate the works of the apostles, but is of no use today, since we now have the written Word of God.

But the gift of speaking in tongues is still as valid today as any of the other gifts of the Holy Spirit, and it is an important part of discipleship. It is such an important gift that the Apostle Paul had a lot to say about it.

The military has always used a secret language, or code, to transmit sensitive information from headquarters to soldiers in the field. Using a code keeps the enemy from knowing what is about to happen. It is much the same with the gift of tongues. When a man speaks in tongues, he speaks in a heavenly language to God, and not to man. I call it our *secret code* with the Father. It is like having a secure, private line to God; a code which the demonic world cannot crack.

Paul says speaking in an unknown tongue edifies or builds up the one doing the speaking. I don't know about you, but I need to be built up and edified in my spirit. Paul goes on to say that he speaks in tongues more than anyone, and wished that everyone spoke in tongues. But Paul didn't *only* pray in tongues. He also prayed in his native language, so his mind could understand.

I learned years ago that if I prayed for everything I could think of, I'd be finished praying in about 15 minutes. But when I started my time with God by praying in the Spirit, before long I would experience another gift of the Spirit, the interpretation of the things I was praying about in the Spirit. The interpretation expanded my range of prayers. I suddenly found a multitude of things to pray over that my natural mind never even considered, and I was able to pray over them with great power.

The Spirit makes intercession for us with groanings, a language that is too deep for us to understand in our natural mind. This is important because the Spirit knows what we need, even if we don't. But when the Holy Spirit gives us the interpretation, we are able to bring our minds into agreement with God's will for our lives. That's a powerful combination.

If you want a strong prayer life you must let the Holy Spirit pray through you. The Apostle Paul understood this. So did the great saints throughout the ages, including my wife, Patti. She is a musician and psalmist. Sometimes she begins to play notes in the Spirit. Those notes become a melody, and she or another person in the gathering will begin to sing in the Spirit. Someone will interpret that spiritual song into our natural English language, and everyone will join in. It is all done decently and in order, and when it happens, it is an awesome experience.

There have been times that we worshiped for hours in the presence of the Lord. He inhabits the praises of His people. When we join with the Holy Spirit and allow Him to use our tongues the way He wants, mighty things happen.

The Holy Spirit won't force you to speak in tongues. It is certainly not an essential component of 'getting saved.' But it is important for building up your faith and edifying your own spirit. With such power and peace, why would you not want to embrace this beautiful gift of the Holy Spirit?

We've kind of touched briefly on the gift of interpretation of tongues. This is a significant gift that often accompanies the gift of speaking in tongues. The gift of tongues for the individual is primarily for his or her own edification, and doesn't always need interpretation when you are alone in your pray closet. But in a public forum, that same unknown tongue doesn't benefit others who can't understand what is being said. The Apostle Paul says if one has a tongue, someone needs to have an interpretation of what is being said in the Spirit so that all there can be edified.

I learned how this works over time. The first time I received an interpretation of tongues was at a church where we were visitors. Someone stood up and spoke in tongues and immediately I knew what they said. I was nervous about giving that interpretation, so I kept it to myself. After a moment of silence another person stood up and gave the exact word I had received.

I felt I had missed my opportunity to minister before the Lord. I told Patti what had happened.

"The Lord will give you another opportunity," she encouraged me.

I wasn't so sure, but He did. Again and again.

Over the years I have become fluent in tongues and interpretations, and you will too once you get started. As we continue daily in communication with the Holy Spirit through our secret code, speaking to the Father in our heavenly language, our thoughts line up with His thoughts and our spirits get in sync with His Spirit.

Don't get discouraged if it takes some time. It really is like becoming fluent in any language. There is no better teacher than the Holy Spirit.

My heart's cry for you is the same as that of the Apostle Paul: *I would not have you be ignorant brethren about the gifts of the Holy Spirit that are given for our common good.*

After reading this brief description of the gifts of the Holy Spirit, it is my sincere hope and prayer that you'll to want to embrace the supernatural working of the Holy Spirit in your life, and accept all the gifts He has for you.

The Holy Spirit confirmed the work of His apostles during the first century by allowing them to perform many mighty miracles, and He is just as active today as He was then. The Holy Spirit still works miracles by the hands of you and me, His present day *Sent Ones*.

Jesus commanded us to go into all the world and make disciples. Mentoring was Jesus' way of crafting disciples, and it's still His way today. No student is greater than his teacher, and you are only as good as you have been mentored yourself. But you can rise above your earthly teachings by studying and learning from the Holy Spirit.

Nourishment for the Journey

I Corinthians 12:1 - *Now concerning spiritual gifts, brethren, I would not have you ignorant.*

Romans 10:17 - *So belief cometh of hearing, and hearing by the word of Christ.*

I Corinthians 12:9, 10 - *To another faith, in the same Spirit; and to another gifts of healings, in the one Spirit; and to another workings of miracles; and to another prophecy; and to another discernings of spirits; to another divers kinds of tongues; and to another the interpretation of tongues.*

I Thessalonians 5:19 - *Quench not the Spirit.*

Acts 1:8 - *But ye shall receive power, when the Holy Spirit is come upon you: and ye shall be my witnesses both in Jerusalem, and in all Judaea and Samaria, and unto the uttermost part of the earth.*

John 14:12 - *Verily, verily, I say unto you, he that believeth on me, the works that I do shall he do also; and greater works than these shall he do; because I go unto the Father.*

John 16:8 - *And he, when he is come, will convict the world in respect of sin, and of righteousness, and of judgment.*

Proverbs 14:34 - *Righteousness exalteth a nation; But sin is a reproach to any people.*

I Corinthians 14:2 - *For he that speaketh in a tongue speaketh not unto men, but unto God; for no man understandeth; but in the spirit he speaketh mysteries.*

Romans 8:26 - *And in like manner the Spirit also helpeth our infirmity: for we know not how to pray as we ought; but the Spirit himself maketh intercession for us with groanings which cannot be uttered.*

Acts 2:38 - *And Peter said unto them, Repent ye, and be baptized every one of you in the name of Jesus Christ unto the remission of your sins; and ye shall receive the gift of the Holy Spirit.*

Chapter 11
How To Know The Voice Of God

People ask me, "How do you know when the Lord is talking to you?"

God speaks to people in a multitude of different ways. Throughout Biblical history and even today He has spoken to individuals and groups of people in an audible voice. One of the most magnificent examples of God speaking audibly for all to hear occurred when Jesus was baptized. God spoke in a voice like thunder proclaiming, *"This is my beloved Son, in whom I am well pleased!"*

At the very beginning of God's interaction with mankind, He spoke audibly. The Genesis account of God walking in the cool of the day with Adam and Eve indicates lengthy discourses between the Creator and His creation. Later, when Adam and Eve disobeyed God by eating the fruit from the tree of the knowledge of good and evil, they tried to hide themselves from the presence of God. Yet, still He called out to them, *"Where are you?"* God wanted to communicate with His fallen creatures then, and He is still calling out to us today.

Let's take a look at an obvious underlying truth from this story. The writer of the New Testament letter to the Hebrews tells us that it is impossible to please God without faith. I believe the first true sin in the Garden of Eden was not the physical eating of the fruit. I believe the original sin was when Eve failed to trust God's voice. She heard the voice of God, but she listened to the voice of another, the serpent. By heeding instructions from a different source, Adam and Eve made another being lord of their lives. Once they realized what they had done, they were ashamed and tried to hide.

Don't be too hard on Adam and Eve. We all do the same thing anytime we trust other people's opinions, or place our fleshly desires over the lordship of Jesus Christ. The result is always feelings of guilt and shame, because of our built-in inner voice called our conscience.

God spoke audibly to Noah instructing him to build an ark to save his family from the impending flood. He spoke to Abram when he was an old man, *"ninety and nine years old,"* and made an amazing promise to him. *"I am God almighty; walk with Me and be blameless. And I will make my covenant between Me and you and will multiply you exceedingly."*

Then, when it looked like God was asking him to give up on that promise by sacrificing his son, Isaac,

God spoke from heaven to Abraham, and delivered the boy.

But God wasn't finished speaking to people. He spoke to Moses from a burning bush. He spoke to Saul of Tarsus from a light so bright it knocked him to the ground and a voice from heaven spoke to him. It's interesting to note that in this event, everyone saw the light, but only Saul, who would later become the Apostle Paul, heard the voice of God.

Perhaps you have never heard the audible voice of God. I'll go out on a limb here and say most folks haven't. But the simple fact that He has not spoken to you in an audible voice, doesn't mean that He cannot or will not do so in the future. His method of communication differs with each of us, and is completely unique and appropriate for His time and purpose.

In my book, **Chronicles of a Believer**, I recount the one time that God spoke to me in an audible voice. He had to speak audibly in order to bring me into the kingdom.

I have walked with Him for over forty years since that day, and He has never chosen to speak audibly to me again. Yet I hear Him speaking to me every day. You can hear his voice, too. As the beloved disciple John says in his Gospel, *"My sheep hear my voice, and I know them and they follow me."*

Sometimes God sends heavenly messengers, called angels, to speak to His people. He used an angel to communicate with Hagar, the mother of Ishmael. He spoke to Abraham through an angel, and gave the promise of a son. That promise sounded so far-fetched to Sarah, who was past the time of childbearing, that she laughed. That's one reason they ended up naming the child, *Isaac* - which means *laughter*.

Angels spoke to many of the mighty prophets and judges of Israel including Balaam, Gideon, Daniel and Elijah. The Lord used His angels to speak to the Virgin Mary about the conception of Jesus, and to Zacharias, about the conception of John the Baptizer. Angels spoke a lot to the Apostle John while he was in exile on the Isle of Patmos. You can read all they said to him in the book of Revelation.

While we must be careful to not worship angels, they are ministering spirits and God still occasionally uses them to communicate with us today. In my book, **Chronicles of a Believer,** I record how two angels appeared to myself and my father-in law in the form of two young men who spoke the word of the Lord to us.

At times God speaks through dreams and visions. This is an entirely Biblical concept. The Apostle Peter declared, *Young men shall see visions and old men shall dream dreams.* The Patriarch Jacob dreamed of a ladder between earth and heaven, with angels ascending and descending by it. The Lord standing at the top as He spoke to him.

Sometimes dreaming can get you into trouble. The patriarch Joseph dreamed that the sun, moon and stars would bow down to him. His brothers didn't like that idea at all, and ended up selling him into slavery. But God is always faithful. Joseph's ability to interpret dreams brought him before Pharaoh, and eventually led to his exaltation as the second highest authority in the land. The prophet Daniel was also an interpreter of dreams and visions, as was also given a great prophetic dream of the end times.

It was in a dream that an angel convinced Joseph that his betrothed wife Mary had not committed adultery. An angel later saved the baby's life by warning Joseph in a dream to flee to Egypt and to later return home. Pilate's wife had a dream, warning him to have nothing to do with the trial of Jesus - good advice that he ignored.

The Roman centurion, Cornelius, had a vision before he was even saved. In his vision, an angel instructed the centurion to send for a man named Simon Peter. Peter was busy having his own vision regarding the nature of clean and unclean things. God used those visions to impart the gospel to the gentiles.

The Apostle Paul had a vision of a man in Macedonia begging him to *"Come over to Macedonia and help us!"*

When God called me to preach, it was through a dream which was confirmed by others within a couple days' time. That story is related in **Chronicles of a Believer**. It is a fun and exciting story about seeing the hand of God at work in our lives.

One of the most common ways God speaks to us, and certainly one way that is accessible to just about everyone, is through His written Word, The Bible. In fact, the written Word of God is the standard against which all other forms of communication from the spirit realm must be judged. If you hear a word that you think might be from God, but it contradicts what is written in the Bible, you can be 100% sure that it was not from God.

That's one very good reason to be thoroughly acquainted with the Bible. The Word of God is powerful, and God is faithful to perform every Word He speaks. God told the prophet Jeremiah that He would watch over the words He gave him to speak, to perform them. Our God is the same today, yesterday and forever. If God gives you a word to speak, don't be afraid to speak it out. He will do it.

The written Word of God *is* God speaking to us. It is trustworthy and true. You can be confident following it, for in doing so you are following Him.

You might never hear the audible voice of God speaking to you. You may never be visited by an angel, or have a prophetic dream or vision. God is still speaking to you. His written Word is His voice to you, and if the Word of God abides in you, then you have overcome the evil one. King David said it this way: *"Thy word have I hid in my heart that I might not sin against God."*

Studying the word of God, and taking it into your heart and mind, will establish an inner sense of His presence. You'll come to know His voice as the Holy Spirit brings to your remembrance what you need, when you need it. I like to call this *programing your computer with the instructions for life.* Just like a computer, if you put nothing in, nothing comes out.

In the words of the Apostle Paul, *"Study to show yourself approved unto God, a workman not needing to be ashamed, rightly dividing the word of truth."*

God can speak to you through other brothers and sisters who have walked faithfully with the Lord. Godly counsel is another good way to determine whether what you've heard is from God. King Solomon, who knew a thing or two about wisdom, encouraged young people to *"Listen to council and accept discipline, that you may be wise the rest of your days."* Wow, that is great advice. Most of what I know and has established me in my faith is the result of wise counsel I received when I was a young believer. It doesn't hurt to seek counsel from more than one mentor. As King Solomon observed, *"Where there is no guidance the people fall, but in the abundance of counselors there is victory."*

Sometimes the encouragement and exhortation we need to help us hear the Word of the Lord clearly comes from being in close proximity to Christian leaders and friends. The writer of the letter to the Hebrews warns us to not forsake assembling together and exhorting each other. Times are tough and it looks like they are getting tougher. As our lives on this planet get more difficult, we'll need each other's love and support even more. No man will stand alone for very long, but with a company of like-minded ones we can endure till the end with great joy.

When our ears become dull to His voice, it is imperative that we are surrounded by others who can still hear clearly until we are able to hear again for ourselves. It was never God's intent that you be a Lone Ranger Christian. From the very beginning God declared that it was not good for man to be alone. Even the world knows how dangerous it is to go it alone. In the Boy Scouts they teach you to 'buddy up!' Never go swimming alone. Never go hunting alone. Never go hiking alone. Never go rock climbing alone. If something goes wrong, and it always does, you could die - alone!

Never try to walk out your faith alone. We were made to need one another.

There is one final way that God speaks to all of His children - through the still small voice of the Holy Spirit, who lives in all believers. The Apostle John, writing to the seven churches in Revelation begged them time and again, *"He who has an ear to hear let him hear what the Spirit is saying."* You can have an ear that hears what the Spirit is saying.

This still small voice, this groaning within you that is too deep for words, this yearning and urging and knowing that you can't deny, is the Holy Spirit speaking to you. Why do you suppose people run to the altar during a revival meeting? Is it just because the preacher was so persuasive? Not at all. Folks are drawn to the altar of God by the urging of the Holy Spirit, the very breath of God within them. Sometimes that urging becomes so strong they simply have to follow it to the altar.

Women may call this knowing deep within them women's intuition. Men may call it a gut feeling. I call it the stirring of the Holy Spirit, and when He urges you, and you trust Him, He is always right.

While God will speak to you, there are plenty of other voices in the spiritual realm vying for your attention. Here are some facts that will help you distinguish which voice is speaking to you. Thoughts of pride, self-exhortation, selfishness, anger, greed or lust are never from the Holy Spirit. If you sense any of these, it's time to start rebuking unclean spirits or even your own flesh. We are commanded by the Word and empowered by the Holy Spirit to take every thought captive to the obedience of Christ.

Thoughts of gentleness, sharing, giving, helping, encouraging, loving, looking for ways to do good for others, putting others ahead of yourself, forgiving, not holding an account against others are all Godly virtues that flow from the voice of the Holy Spirit. Being obedient to these will deliver joy to your spirit.

Knowing Jesus as our Savior creates the bridge from our fallen state to His Father's Kingdom. But making Him Lord is vitally important if we want to live successful, productive lives in the physical realm. Making Jesus Lord requires us to hear and understand His voice, and to distinguish it from the voice of the adversary and from the voice of our own fleshly desires. For that, we need the indwelling power of the Holy Spirit.

Nourishment for the Journey

John 10:27 - *My sheep hear my voice, and I know them, and they follow me.*

Genesis 2:15-17 - *And Jehovah God took the man, and put him into the garden of Eden to dress it and to keep it. And Jehovah God commanded the man, saying, Of every tree of the garden thou mayest freely eat: but of the tree of the knowledge of good and evil, thou shalt not eat of it: for in the day that thou eatest thereof thou shalt surely die.*

Hebrews 11:6 - *And without faith it is impossible to be well-pleasing unto him; for he that cometh to God must believe that he is, and that he is a rewarder of them that seek after him.*

Genesis 7:1 - *And Jehovah said unto Noah, Come thou and all thy house into the ark; for thee have I seen righteous before me in this generation.*

Genesis 17:1 - *And when Abram was ninety years old and nine, Jehovah appeared to Abram, and said unto him, I am God Almighty; walk before me, and be thou perfect.*

Genesis 22:11 - *And the angel of Jehovah called unto him out of heaven, and said, Abraham, Abraham. And he said, Here I am.*

Acts 7:31-32 - *And when Moses saw it, he wondered at the sight: and as he drew near to behold, there came a voice of the Lord, I am the God of thy fathers, the God of Abraham, and of Isaac, and of Jacob. And Moses trembled, and durst not behold.*

Acts 9:3-7 - *And as he journeyed, it came to pass that he drew nigh unto Damascus: and suddenly there shone round about him a light out of heaven: and he fell upon the earth, and heard a voice saying unto him, Saul, Saul, why persecutest thou me? And he said, Who art thou, Lord? And he said, I am Jesus whom thou persecutest: but rise, and enter into the city, and it shall be told thee what thou must do. And the men that journeyed with him stood speechless, hearing the voice, but beholding no man.*

Matthew 3:17 - *And lo, a voice out of the heavens, saying, This is my beloved Son, in whom I am well pleased.*

Genesis 16:9-11 - *And the angel of Jehovah said unto her, Return to thy mistress, and submit thyself under her hands. And the angel of Jehovah said unto her, I will greatly multiply thy seed, that it shall not be numbered for multitude. And the angel of Jehovah said unto her, Behold, thou art with child, and shalt bear a son; and thou shalt call his name Ishmael, because Jehovah hath heard thy affliction.*

Genesis 8:17 - *Bring forth with thee every living thing that is with thee of all flesh, both birds, and cattle, and every creeping thing that creepeth upon the earth; that they may breed abundantly in the earth, and be fruitful, and multiply upon the earth.*

Genesis 26:2-5, 24 - *And Jehovah appeared unto him, and said, Go not down into Egypt. Dwell in the land which I shall tell thee of. Sojourn in this land, and I will be with thee, and will bless thee. For unto thee, and unto thy seed, I will give all these lands, and I will* *establish the oath which I sware unto Abraham thy father. And I will multiply thy seed as the stars of heaven, and will give unto thy seed all these lands. And in thy seed shall all the nations of the earth be blessed. Because that Abraham obeyed my voice, and kept my charge, my commandments, my statutes, and my laws... And Jehovah appeared unto him the same night, and said, I am the God of Abraham thy father. Fear not, for I am with thee, and will bless thee, and multiply thy seed for my servant Abraham's sake.*

Acts 2:17 - *And it shall be in the last days, saith God, I will pour forth of my Spirit upon all flesh: And your sons and your daughters shall prophesy, And your young men shall see visions, And your old men shall dream dreams.*

Genesis 31:3 - *And Jehovah said unto Jacob, Return unto the land of thy fathers, and to thy kindred; and I will be with thee.*

Daniel 1:17 - *Now as for these four youths, God gave them knowledge and skill in all learning and wisdom: and Daniel had understanding in all visions and dreams.*

Daniel 7:1 - *In the first year of Belshazzar king of Babylon Daniel had a dream and visions of his head upon his bed: then he wrote the dream and told the sum of the matters.*

Matthew 1:20-21 - *But when he thought on these things, behold, an angel of the Lord appeared unto him in a dream, saying, Joseph, thou son of David, fear not to take unto thee Mary thy wife: for that which is* *conceived in her is of the Holy Spirit. And she shall bring forth a son; and thou shalt call his name JESUS; for it is he that shall save his people from their sins.*

Matthew 27:19 - *And while he was sitting on the judgment-seat, his wife sent unto him, saying, Have thou nothing to do with that righteous man; for I have suffered many things this day in a dream because of him.*

Acts 10:36 - *The word which he sent unto the children of Israel, preaching good tidings of peace by Jesus Christ (He is Lord of all.)*

Acts 16:9 - *And a vision appeared to Paul in the night: There was a man of Macedonia standing, beseeching him, and saying, Come over into Macedonia, and help us.*

Psalm 103:20 - *Bless Jehovah, ye his angels, That are mighty in strength, that fulfil his word, Hearkening unto the voice of his word.*

Jeremiah 1:12 - *Then said Jehovah unto me, Thou hast well seen: for I watch over my word to perform it.*

I John 2:5 - *but whoso keepeth his word, in him verily hath the love of God been perfected. Hereby we know that we are in him.*

I John 2:14 - *I have written unto you, fathers, because ye know him who is from the beginning. I have written unto you, young men, because ye are strong, and the word of God abideth in you, and ye have overcome the evil one.*

Psalm 119:11 - *Thy word have I laid up in my heart, That I might not sin against thee.*

2 Timothy 2:15 - *Give diligence to present thyself approved unto God, a workman that needeth not to be ashamed, handling aright the word of truth.*

Proverbs 19:20 - *Hear counsel, and receive instruction, That thou mayest be wise in thy latter end.*

Proverbs 22:6 - *Train up a child in the way he should go, And even when he is old he will not depart from it.*

Proverbs 11:14 - *Where no wise guidance is, the people falleth; But in the multitude of counsellors there is safety.*

Hebrews 10:25 - *Not forsaking our own assembling together, as the custom of some is, but exhorting one another; and so much the more, as ye see the day drawing nigh.*

John 10:27 - *My sheep hear my voice, and I know them, and they follow me.*

Revelation 2:7 - *He that hath an ear, let him hear what the Spirit saith to the churches. To him that overcometh, to him will I give to eat of the tree of life, which is in the Paradise of God.*

John 7:38 - *He that believeth on me, as the scripture hath said, from within him shall flow rivers of living water.*

Proverbs 20:27 - *The spirit of man is the lamp of Jehovah, Searching all his innermost parts.*

I Corinthians 2:11-13 - *For who among men knoweth the things of a man, save the spirit of the man, which is in him? even so the things of God none knoweth, save the Spirit of God. But we received, not the spirit of the world, but the spirit which is from God;*

that we might know the things that were freely given to us of God. Which things also we speak, not in words which man's wisdom teacheth, but which the Spirit teacheth; combining spiritual things with spiritual words.

Chapter 12
Be Strong In The Lord

Jesus told Peter He would give him the keys of the kingdom of heaven, and whatever he would bind on earth would be bound in heaven, and whatever he loosed on earth would be loosed in heaven.

This whole 'binding' and 'loosing' thing really is just another term for spiritual warfare, and to battle successfully requires power. The same power that raised Christ from the dead, and that Christ offered to Peter, is available to us through the Holy Spirit. He is One who helps us to overcome this world system on a day-in, day-out basis. And make no mistake - this spiritual battle we fight is a battle daily. It requires us to be constantly on our guard against the wiles of the devil. We must be fully dressed for battle, both to defend and to attack.

The Apostle Paul encouraged the Ephesian believers to be strong in the Lord and the power of His might. I want to give you that same encouragement today. We can be strong, but only in

His might, not in our own. He has already given us every resource we need to be not just strong, but mighty, to the pulling down of strongholds!

We need those spiritual resources, those disciplines, because we're not wrestling against physical adversaries. Our quarrel is not with flesh and blood human beings, but with principalities, powers, against the rulers of darkness of this world, against hosts of spiritual wickedness in heavenly places. That kind of enemy doesn't easily bow the knee, and it certainly doesn't cower to mere human strength. That's why it is imperative that we put on the full armor of God.

The full armor of God will cause us to stand, and not fold when the going gets tough. You don't go to work in your pajamas, and you shouldn't attempt to resist the devil in your spiritual underwear. Putting on His armor is like getting dressed spiritually.

It starts by wrapping the belt of truth around your waist. Jesus said, *"I am the Truth."* The Word of God is truth. The truth will set us free. God wants us to know the truth, and to tell the truth, because the truth will set those who hear it free.

The Word is full of authority or jurisdiction over the problem at hand. The Word is law, establish by God to stand forever and ever. The truth of God's Word will deliver us, but only if you know the truth. Putting on the belt of truth involves studying, meditating and confessing His word above all other thoughts and imaginations of your heart. One important truth about God's Word is that you will never outgrow your need for delving into it. It is a rich storehouse. The more you dwell in it, the more you will learn from it.

Next, put on the breastplate of righteousness and the helmet of salvation. Most of your vital organs - your heart, your lungs, you stomach, your liver, your kidneys, your intestines - are contained in your torso. Your means of communication - your brain, your eyes, ears and mouth - are exposed in your head. In the old days, soldiers wore a breastplate and helmet to protect those vital organs against blows from their enemy.

Our spiritual enemy, Satan, attacks us ferociously with fiery darts of accusations, lies, bitterness, jealously and distrust of God and others. Righteousness, which comes from a right relationship with God, acts as armor against such offenses. Be careful to not rely on your own righteousness. Scripture is very clear that our own righteousness is like filthy rags; it won't protect you against any attack of the enemy. That's where the helmet of salvation comes in. Salvation imparts Jesus' righteousness to us.

Putting on the breastplate of righteousness involves intentionally and continually choosing to love and forgive. It involves seeking to do the right thing in each and every situation we encounter. Being righteous before the Lord is like putting on a spiritual bulletproof vest. The enemy cannot beat you if you cannot be wounded with offense.

Lace up your work boots of the gospel of peace. Some Roman Legionnaires had spikes on the bottom of their boots that they could embed into the ground to help them keep sound footing on slippery slopes, and to help them hold their position when pressed in battle. It is a paradox that we must fight for peace, and that one of the weapons of our warfare is peace itself. But the truth is, the gospel, the good news of Jesus Christ, is His peace that passes all understanding. This peace, if you put it on each day, will guard our hearts and minds, and allow you to stand firm when all else is giving way around you.

As in the natural, you will never win a defensive war. The best you can hope for is a stalemate, and who wants a stalemate with the devil? At some point you have to take the offensive, and that means picking up the shield of faith and the sword of the Spirit, which is the Word of God.

The shield is both a defensive armor and an offensive weapon. It protects you as you move forward to take ground from the adversary. Taking that ground means rightly wielding the sword of the Spirit. The Word of God is like a sharp double-edged sword that is able to divide truth from lies, light from darkness and even the soul from the spirit. As with any weapon, it can be extremely dangerous if not wielded properly and with skill. You can even wound your own comrades with it if you are not careful. That's just one more reason to study to show yourself approved.

Nourishment for the Journey

John 16:19 - *Jesus perceived that they were desirous to ask him, and he said unto them, Do ye inquire among yourselves concerning this, that I said, A little while, and ye behold me not, and again a little while, and ye shall see me?*

Ephesians 6:10-18 - *Finally, be strong in the Lord, and in the strength of his might. Put on the whole armor of God, that ye may be able to stand against the wiles of the devil. For our wrestling is not against flesh and blood, but against the principalities, against the powers, against the world-rulers of this darkness, against the spiritual hosts of wickedness in the heavenly places. Wherefore take up the whole armor of God, that ye may be able to withstand in the evil day, and, having done all, to stand. Stand therefore, having girded your loins with truth, and having put on the breastplate of righteousness, and having shod your feet with the preparation of the gospel of peace; withal taking up the shield of faith, wherewith ye shall be able to quench all the fiery darts of the evil one. And take the helmet of salvation, and the sword of the Spirit, which is the word of God: with all prayer and supplication praying at all seasons in the Spirit, and watching thereunto in all perseverance and supplication for all the saints.*

Colossians 3:15 - *And let the peace of Christ rule in your hearts, to the which also ye were called in one body; and be ye thankful.*

Philippians 2:10 - *that in the name of Jesus every knee should bow, of things in heaven and things on earth and things under the earth.*

Chapter 13
Build A Strong House

Just hearing Jesus' words won't do you much good. You have to act on them. Jesus told a parable about a man who built his house on the sand, and when the wind and rains came, that house crumbled because it had no foundation. A wise man, on the other hand, builds his house on a firm foundation, a rock. This man doesn't have to worry about the wind and the rain. His house will stand through the storms. Jesus went on to explain that His Word was the rock that we must build our lives on. If we just hear the Word, but don't act on it, we're like that guy who built his house on the sand.

Just like the men in that parable, there are only two options for how you live your life. You can follow the instruction manual, the Holy Bible, which leads to a sound and successful life, or you can follow the world's way and indulge the lust of the flesh the lust of the eye and the pride of life. The problem is, the way of the world leads to a sure collapse once the storms of life come, which they surely will.

Rome and your home weren't built in a day, and neither is your spiritual house. In fact, building your spiritual house is a continual process that takes a lifetime, and it requires a daily decision making process. You might as well know right up front that you are going to make some bad decisions. Some days you might not hear as well as you want, other days you might not even listen for the voice of God. Still other days you might even intentionally choose to do things that are contrary to the Word of God.

The days we choose to obey produce good fruit, while the days we ignore Him produce fruit that is not fit to eat. Consider the nation of Israel throughout the Old Testament. When they obeyed the Word of the Lord, they prospered. When they ignored or disobeyed God, they went into captivity.

I can attest that in my own life, when I obeyed, I prospered. But when I embraced the Frank Sinatra mentality and *did it my way,* it always cost me.

Fortunately, the Lord makes provision for us even when we mess up. There is a wonderful verse that declares, *Many are the afflictions of the righteous but the Lord delivers us out of them all.* Remember, our righteousness does not come from our actions, but is imparted to us through faith in the completed work of Jesus Christ.

But as wonderful as that promise of rescue is, it is even more wonderful that we can avoid the snares of the adversary by choosing wisely. The only way to choose wisely is to become wise, and the only way to become wise is by studying the Word and relying on the Holy Spirit to reveal truth. The Apostle Paul encouraged his young protégé Timothy (and us) to study to show ourselves approved unto God, workmen who don't need to be ashamed because we are able to rightly divide the word of truth.

In other words, we need to be craftsmen of the faith, skilled laborers who can both perform the works of righteousness and train others to follow our example. We can become good at being disciples. It takes work, but that work brings Him glory and us victory.

This thing of being crafted into a disciple is more involved than just being baptized in water. It is learning to fully embrace the heavenly Father as your Father, and fully embracing the Jesus as the Truth - your Truth, your Way and your Life.

Jesus came that you can have abundant life, but while salvation is free, it is not cheap. He must become Lord of all in regard to your life and what you do with it. He is the master planner of your course and the master builder of your destiny. But you won't know the wonder of it unless you fully follower His direction given through the Word and the Holy Spirit.

You must fully embrace all of the Holy Spirit to have a full, strong and successful life. It is the Holy Spirit that will help you build your spiritual house upon the Rock, so no amount of wind, rain, hail and crashing waves of life can cause it to collapse.

The control to your success as a disciple of Jesus Christ is in your hands. It is yours to decide on a daily basis, and no one can do that for you. If you do your part by surrendering to Him, He will do His part, and walk with you always - even to the end of the earth.

Nourishment for the Journey

Matthew 7:21-27 - *Not every one that saith unto me, Lord, Lord, shall enter into the kingdom of heaven; but he that doeth the will of my Father who is in heaven. Many will say to me in that day, Lord, Lord, did we not prophesy by thy name, and by thy name cast out demons, and by thy name do many mighty works? And then will I profess unto them, I never knew you: depart from me, ye that work iniquity. Every one therefore that heareth these words of mine, and doeth them, shall be likened unto a wise man, who built his house upon the rock: and the rain descended, and the floods came, and the winds blew, and beat upon that house; and it fell not: for it was founded upon the rock. And every one that heareth these words of mine, and doeth them not, shall be likened unto a foolish man, who built his house upon the sand: and the rain descended, and the floods came, and the winds blew, and smote upon that house; and it fell: and great was the fall thereof.*

2 Timothy 2:15 - *Give diligence to present thyself approved unto God, a workman that needeth not to be ashamed, handling aright the word of truth.*

Matthew 28:20 - *teaching them to observe all things whatsoever I commanded you: and lo, I am with you always, even unto the end of the world.*

Chapter 14
The Life Of Prayer

We must be in constant communication with the Father. There is a popular notion that only those prayers that are said in your private, secret prayer closet will find their way to God. After all, Jesus did encourage people to pray in secret and the Father who sees in secret will reward you openly.

But that's only part of the story. Jesus wasn't really teaching about prayer as much as our motivation to pray. He was condemning praying in public so that people would esteem you for your holiness. If all you are looking for is the praise of men, you'll get that reward, but you'll miss true intimacy with God.

Communicating with God isn't a religious formula, nor is having an intimate relationship with him something spooky or unnatural. I like the Old Testament story about Enoch. He walked with God and talked with God on a regular basis. He had such a wonderfully intimate relationship with God that one day, while he and God were walking and talking together, he discovered he was closer to God's house than he was to his own. In fact, he walked so closely to God that he wasn't found on earth anymore, for God took him home to be with Him.

The writer of the letter to the Hebrews says that Enoch's faith was so great that God translated him, and he did not see death. Imagine having such a close relationship with God that you don't have to taste death in order to pass into life. That kind of event is only recorded about two people, Enoch and the prophet Elijah, who was caught up into heaven in a fiery chariot. What a goal for us; to have such an intimate relationship with God that He would just take us from earth to be with Him.

That kind of intimacy only comes by spending time in the presence of the Lord. That involves increasing our faith by hearing the word and having daily conversations with our Heavenly Father through the process called prayer.

You can certainly pray in your private, secret place, much like you can carry on a quiet, intimate conversation with your spouse at night when you've gone to bed. But I'll bet you don't stop talking to your spouse in the morning after the kids are awake. You continue to communicate with one another, both verbally and sometimes non-verbally.

You can, and should, continue to communicate with the Father all day long. Just talk to Him. About everything. Just like you would if your best friend was riding shotgun on your way to work. And just like if your best friend was with you, don't do all the talking. Take some time to listen to what the Father is saying to you through the Spirit. It's not spooky. It's the most normal thing in the world.

You'll find as you both speak and listen to God in conversational prayer, He will fill your spirit with understanding and knowledge, and more than that, His Holy Spirit will lead you to higher ground.

God is interested in your success in His Kingdom, but success doesn't necessarily look the same to Him as it does to us. Think about the great people of faith in the New Testament. Many of them were beaten, arrested, ridiculed and even executed for their faith. That doesn't look like success in our eyes, but the death of His saints is precious in the eyes of the Lord.

To understand true success we must listen to Him. It takes time to get to know Him; lots of time. But it's worth it. Jesus commanded us to seek first the Kingdom of God and then all these things will be added to you. Seeking is not a one time event; it's progressive. Seek and keep on seeking. Knock and keep on knocking. Ask and keep on asking.

The Old Testament prophet, Jeremiah, uttered one of the most quoted verses in the Bible when he said by the Holy Spirit, *"I know the plans I have for you, declares the Lord, plans to prosper you and not to harm you, plans to give you hope and a future. Then you will call on me and come and pray to me and I will listen to you. You will seek me and find me when you seek me with all your heart."* (Jeremiah 29: 11-13 NIV)

What an offer! How can anyone pass up this deal? We who are weak can be made strong. We who are lost can be found. We who are lonely can have a friend that sticks closer than a brother. He who was rich became poor so that we who are poor could become rich. He took our sin and unrighteousness upon Himself, and exchanged it for right standing with God for us. He took our penalty of death upon Himself to set us free from sin and death. He is the Father to the fatherless, the comforter to those walking in fear and anxiety. He is the author and finisher of our faith. He is crafting us daily into His image, if we are spending quality time with Him.

Our Heavenly Father has made Himself available to us through the person of Jesus Christ that we may come boldly to His throne of grace at any time. Daily conversation with the Father, the Son and the Holy Spirit is the key to being fashioned into a true disciple of Christ.

Nourishment for the Journey

Hebrews 11:5, 6 - *By faith Enoch was translated that he should not see death; and he was not found, because God translated him: for he hath had witness borne to him that before his translation he had been well-pleasing unto God: And without faith it is impossible to be well-pleasing unto him; for he that cometh to God must believe that he is, and that he is a rewarder of them that seek after him.*

I Peter 5:6 - *Humble yourselves therefore under the mighty hand of God, that he may exalt you in due time.*

Matthew 6:33 - *But seek ye first his kingdom, and his righteousness; and all these things shall be added unto you.*

Matthew 7:7 - *Ask, and it shall be given you; seek, and ye shall find; knock, and it shall be opened unto you.*

Jeremiah 29:11 - *For I know the thoughts that I think toward you, saith Jehovah, thoughts of peace, and not of evil, to give you hope in your latter end.*

Hebrews 12:1, 2 - *Therefore let us also, seeing we are compassed about with so great a cloud of witnesses, lay aside every weight, and the sin which doth so easily beset us, and let us run with patience the race that is set before us, looking unto Jesus the author and perfecter of our faith, who for the joy that was set before him endured the cross, despising shame, and hath sat down at the right hand of the throne of God.*

Ephesians 6:18 - *With all prayer and supplication praying at all seasons in the Spirit, and watching thereunto in all perseverance and supplication for all the saints.*

Conclusion

We need to be coached by others in the faith, so we can become skilled followers of Jesus Christ. As we grow in faith we are encouraged to be filled with the power and knowledge of how the kingdom of God works. We become skilled at applying those truths to our daily walk. As we grow into a skilled master craftsman of the Kingdom, we are called to coach and mentor others to follow in His footsteps.

You are called to be an apprentice of Jesus Christ, a disciple, a true follower of His way, truth and life. What you have learned from Christ, you are to impart to others - first in your own circle of acquaintences, and then on the broader scale until we reach out to the uttermost parts of the world.

The first step along this journey is accepting Christ as your Lord and Savior, then growing in faith by walking with Him daily as the author and finisher of your faith. This involves commitment and self-discipline to daily study His word, to daily communicate with Him through conversational prayer and to keep yourself in right relationship with the Father by confessing your sins and asking for forgiveness of transgressions against His Kingdom. The journey continues when we listen to His voice, walk in His presence and acknowledge Him in all our ways.

Consider Him in all your decisions, then do what He directs you to do. And remember His promise to never leave you. He will be with you to the very end of the earth.

It all starts by accepting Jesus Christ as your Lord and Savior. If you have not accepted Him into your life, won't you come? You can do that right now by simply praying this prayer.

Jesus, I believe you are the Son of God, that you died on the cross for my sins; that your Father raised you from the dead and you are now seated at the right hand of Father God. I ask you to become my Lord right now and forgive me of my sins.

If you have just prayed that prayer for the first time or hundredth, you are accepted into the family of God and the Holy Spirit now dwells within you. I suggest going back and studying this book again through the eyes of the Spirit, and learn how to be a true follower of Christ. I guarantee you that His peace and joy will be with you to your journey's end.

Blessing,
Brother Don

Special Thanks

I would like to give my special thanks to my close friend and publisher Mike Parker, for all of his hard work and creative direction in bringing forth this book. His participation in this book is exactly what I was sharing on how our gifts work together for the common good of the body.

Don McCain

Check Out These Inspirational Titles from WordCrafts Press

(www.wordcrafts.net)

Never Run A Dead Kata
    (Lessons I learned in the Dojo)
by Rodney Boyd

Why I Failed in the Music Business
    (and how NOT to follow in my footsteps)
by Steve Grossman

Youth Ministry is Easy!
    (and 9 other lies)
by Aaron Shaver

A Scarlet Cord of Hope
by Sheryl Griffin

Illuminations
by Paula K. Parker & Tracy Sugg

Chronicles of a Believer
by Don McCain